745.1
Str
Stratton
Mugs and tankards   9.95

THE PUBLIC LIBRARY OF DES MOINES
3 1704 0034 9854 0

FRANKLIN AVE. LIBRARY
MAY YOU ENJOY THIS BOOK

DO *NOT* REMOVE THE "DATE DUE"
CARD FROM THIS POCKET

Books may be returned to the Main Library, the branches or bookmobiles regardless of where they were checked out. Please return books promptly so that others may enjoy them.

**THE PUBLIC LIBRARY
OF DES MOINES, IOWA**

The processing of this
material is partially
paid for by the State
Library Commission of
Iowa with federal funds.

MUGS AND TANKARDS

MUGS AND TANKARDS

by
Deborah Stratton

SOUVENIR PRESS

Copyright © 1975 by Deborah Stratton

First published 1975 by Souvenir Press Ltd.,
43 Great Russell Street, London WC1B 3PA
and simultaneously in Canada by
J. M. Dent & Sons (Canada) Ltd.,
Ontario, Canada.

All Rights Reserved. No part of this publication
may be reproduced, stored in a retrieval system,
or transmitted, in any form or by any means, electronic,
mechanical, photocopying, recording or otherwise, without
the prior permission of the Copyright owner.

ISBN 0 285 62186 6

Printed in Great Britain by E. J. Arnold & Son Limited, Leeds

TABLE OF CONTENTS

ACKNOWLEDGEMENTS		6
PREFACE		7
CHAPTER 1	Beer and Britannia	9
CHAPTER 2	Silver Mugs and Tankards	22
CHAPTER 3	Pewter Mugs and Tankards	39
CHAPTER 4	Pottery Mugs and Tankards	61
CHAPTER 5	Porcelain Mugs and Tankards	93
CHAPTER 6	Glass, Leather and Wooden Mugs and Tankards	115
BIBLIOGRAPHY		136
INDEX		139

ACKNOWLEDGEMENTS

I would like to thank Mr. Arthur Binsted of the Brewer's Society for his help on the background to ale and beer drinking and the following dealers and auctioneers who provided me with photographs and/or information; of whom Jennifer May, Geoffrey Godden, Richard Mundey, Sue Rose of Christie's, Richard Dennis and his assistant were particularly generous with their time:

Christie, Manson and Woods
Sotheby & Co.
Robert Williams of Winifred Williams
Richard Dennis
Christopher Sykes
Richard Mundey
Jennifer and John May
Phillips
John Brooks
Walter Parrish International (who created *The Collectors' Encyclopedia of Antiques*)
The Corning Museum of Glass
Walsall Museum
W. G. T. Burne
Independent Magazines (publishers of *Art and Antiques Weekly*)

London Museum
Garrard & Co. Ltd.
Gerald Benney
Association of British Pewter Craftsmen
Whitefriars Glass
N. Bloom and Son Ltd.
Geoffrey Godden, chinaman
Messenger May Baverstock
King and Chasemore
Riddett and Adams Smith
Sworders
Geoffrey Harley
Wedgwood
Coalport
Henry Spencer & Sons
The Worshipful Co. of Pewterers

PREFACE

The custom of meeting one's friends at the local pub is as old as the Saxons, but drinking at home was for most of our history far more customary than drinking out as the British do today. Thus a great many different types of vessels were made for the consumption of beer, ale, cider, wine, mead and spirits in the privacy of one's home. Even when travelling, people often took their alcoholic drinks with them.

By and large, the mug or tankard held ale, beer, porter, mead or cider and was made of wood, leather, pottery, porcelain, glass, silver or pewter. In inns and taverns hardy inexpensive materials such as wood, leather, pewter and stoneware were used to enable the carousing clientele to enjoy their drinks without causing constant breakages. While at home, in the refined days of the 18th century particularly, glass, porcelain and silver were much preferred by those who could afford them. Then as pewter became expensive and acquired prestige in the late 19th century, it too was used at home by the well-to-do, and in public drinking places industrialized pub glass came in to replace it.

A word about terms. To me a tankard has a lid and a mug does not. Some people like to make mugs sound grander by calling them tankards, possibly using the excuse that a large lidless vessel is a tankard and a smaller one a mug. But usage is sloppy and I prefer to set the record straight, justifying my terminology on the grounds that most silver experts are clear about the distinction, whereas writers on ceramics and glass and pewter are inconsistent. In this book, then, a lidless drinking vessel with a handle is a mug, a lidded drinking vessel with a handle is a tankard, and a drinking vessel with a handle that once had a lid is a lidless tankard.

Chapter One
BEER AND BRITANNIA

Ale has warmed the hearts and inspired the minds of the British for approximately 3000 years. Whether drunk from skins, pottery, wood, pewter, glass or silver, it has quenched thirst, spread conviviality and, most important of all, fostered friendship, literature, discussion, debate and self-government.

Grandiose claims for an alcoholic drink made from barley, malt (or other grain such as wheat), yeast and water, with herbs or later hops to flavour it? No, the forerunner of the English pub was the principal meeting place where, because water was none too safe to drink and the roads were hazardous at night, people stopped for sustenance and rest – and in the process exchanged information and views as well as friendly greetings.

Ale is probably as old as man's ability to use the products of the soil. Certainly bread and ale were two of the earliest man-made foods. They were even once created by similar processes. In Mesopotamia some 6000 years ago ale was made by mashing a special bread with a barley malt and leaving it to ferment.

Drawings in Egypt about the same time show people drinking ale and even revering it by offering it up to their gods. Noah took beer with him on the ark.

The evidence is that ale was brewed in Britain at least from the first century. The ingredients were available: there is a British coin of this period showing an ear of cultivated barley on one side, and Julius Caesar, who landed in Britain in the summer of 55 BC, made frequent references to the cultivation of cereal crops. Certainly by the first century AD Pliny the Elder, Roman author and historian, was writing of drinks made from barley in Western Europe which caused drunkenness. In his words, 'The whole world is addicted to drunkenness; the perverted ingenuity of man has given to water the power of intoxicating where wine is not procurable. Western nations intoxicate themselves by means of moistened grain.'[1]

The Saxons in the 5th and 6th centuries AD met in alehouses and there debated issues and decided their laws. And in the centuries following the arrival of Augustine in England in 597 AD to preach Christianity, the church too assumed an interest in the taverns and alehouses. Ecbright, Archbishop of York in the 8th century, insisted on accommodation being provided by the church as the taverns and alehouses had unsavoury reputations. And in the 10th century there were so many drinking establishments that Edgar the Peaceful, King of England, decreed that they should be restricted to one for each village.

Ale has been the national beverage since earliest times. Even the Magna Carta of 1215 included in its terms the provision that there should be a standard measure for ale (and also for wine, as under the Norman influence much wine was shipped to England from France). The great wit the Rev. Sydney Smith (1771–1845), the man who wrote 'I never read a book before reviewing it, it prejudices a man so', also said in *The Smith of Smiths*, 'What two ideas are more inseparable than Beer and Britannia?'

By 1393 the tradition of a pictorial signboard outside every inn was well-established in order to guide travellers to shelter and in that year Richard II decreed that publicans who brewed their own ale should display a sign to enable the ale inspector to come and taste it. Illiteracy was, of course, the rule rather than the exception, so the sign of the bull and the bush had to be relied on to tell you where you were. Thus has the fascinating tradition of pub signs developed, giving us such wonderful collector's items as the 'Cat and Custard Pot', the 'Drunken Duck' and the 'Dog and Bacon'.

When the monasteries not only brewed the ale but provided the inns, they had often to procure additional buildings for lodging travellers, which accounts for the village establishment called 'The New Inn' which dates back to the Middle Ages! 'Inn' is an Anglo-Saxon word meaning a room or hall.

---

[1] 'A Historical Survey of English Ale, Beer and Public Houses', H. A. Monckton, *Brewers' Guild Journal*, September 1968.

The monasteries became known as the best brewers in Europe because they found the sources of the best waters. Part of the brewing process involved boiling, and ale could, therefore, be drunk with impunity, whereas one would hesitate to drink water unless one knew where it came from.

Ale was sometimes used as barter, or for meeting the rent. It was also sold by the church. And the word 'bridal' comes from the Anglo-Saxon 'brydeolo' meaning bride-ale, for the bride used to provide ale for her guests in return for wedding presents.

By the end of the 12th century English ale was known abroad, for it was said of two ecclesiastics by the Pope that they had entered into a dispute through 'drinking too much English ale'.

In February 1400, 'bière' came to England from the Continent where it was flavoured with hops. The locals, as ever reluctant to change, resisted the idea of substituting hops for the local herbs such as thyme and rosemary, which had served them very well. Henry VIII loved sweet and stong ales brewed from malt, yeast and water and banned the use of hops. Brewers were still resisting it in the 17th century; but by the end of the century about two

Lambeth delft mug inscribed "Thomas Hunt of Eden 1635." This very rare item of early English delft has a mottled manganese glaze. *Photograph: Winifred Williams.*

million barrels of beer were being produced annually and strong brews, costing about 16s. a barrel, were being lightly hopped. Weaker 'small' beer was about 6s. a barrel. There were some 199 brewers in London alone in the latter part of the 17th century, and by that time English beer was so famous that it was outlawed in parts of Germany (although those who could get hold of it, such as innkeepers, continued to imbibe freely).

For a long time the use of hops caused a distinction to be made between beer and ale, but eventually hops figured in the brewing of both, and beer and ale became synonymous. In 1607, when instead of the convivial 'pint of beer' taken today, it was more likely to be 'a quart of ale', a quart of strong ale or two quarts of small beer could be bought for one penny.

Although the richer people sometimes treated themselves to wine from France, ale was the universal drink of all Englishmen throughout later Christian times and the Middle Ages. In the 17th century, however, it came into increasing competition with brandy, port, sherry and other wines, primarily among the wealthier classes.

Ale was taxed for the first time in 1640 by Cromwell, and this undoubtedly aided the popularity of other alcoholic drinks. In 1692 the tax was increased in order to stimulate the sale of spirits, an action that was later regretted, especially when the evils perpetuated by cheap gin became plain to the eye. Bottled beer was available, but not in great demand.

From the beginning of the 18th century it was required by law that beer (I now employ this as a universal term for all kinds of beer and ale) be sold in mugs or tankards officially measured and stamped with the measures on them. A collector will, therefore, look for signs of these measures. I should mention at this point that, although this book is about mugs and tankards, I do not think a collector will turn down the opportunity to buy any of the magnificent flagons that were used for containing large amounts of the liquid for pouring into the pint, quart, or whatever, container. Nor will he necessarily exclude the attractive measures that marched in sloping formation behind the bar, such as the famous Scottish Tappit Hens with their concave waists, or the more common baluster shapes.

There are certainly instances anyway in which functions overlapped. Mr Arthur Binsted of the Brewers' Society recently measured items from the splendid collection of beer vessels of the Worshipful Company of Goldsmiths at Goldsmith's Hall in London. He found a number of odd measures amounting to more than the usual pint or quart, and his theory is that many silver and silver gilt tankards were used on high days and holidays as serving tankards during the 16th to 18th centuries. The people may actually have drunk from pottery or pewter or small silver mugs of approximately half or full pint capacity.

Douglas Ash in the *Dictionary of British Antique Silver*[2] gives the definition of flagon as 'a name which began to be applied in the early 17th century to a kind of tall tankard of large capacity, previously known as a livery pot, which was used either for drinking or for serving liquor into smaller vessels. Large silver flasks were also sometimes called flagons.' This puts flagons into such close kinship with tankards as to make them eligible for inclusion in this book.

The origin of the term 'to take down a peg' comes from the 'peg tankards' in use from the Middle Ages. People used to go to inns and challenge or invite each other to drink each other down to one of the pegs fastened inside the tankard; or else, sharing out a peg tankard, mete out the beverage fairly by each drinking down to a peg.

By the same token, one could 'drink a merrie pin', a later expression which comes from the North of England where Scandinavian-type silver peg-tankards were in use. With the pegs or 'pins' set at equal distances from the top to the bottom, one would aim, when drinking in fellowship, to drink down to a peg without looking before passing the tankard on. Inexperienced drinkers who failed to gauge the distance were required to drink to the next peg and if they still did not end on a pin might have to drink the whole lot. This way they became 'high' and were said to have 'drunk a merrie pin.'

---

[2] *Dictionary of British Antique Silver*, Douglas Ash, Pelham Books, pp. 93–94.

Besides being associated with Roman gladiatorial combat, the expression 'thumbs up' has its place in beer-drinking history. It is said that in the great houses at mealtimes, gentility prevailed when ladies discreetly signalled to the butler by the thumbs up sign if they wanted strong beer and thumbs down if they wanted the weaker.

In 1727 the term 'porter' came in, being a ready-mixed drink of ale and beer, and 'tuppenny', which was something in between ale and beer. Before porter was ready-mixed (and termed 'entire'), many drinkers requested 'half and half' (ale and beer) or 'two-thirds' (a combination of the three). Ale was by that time costing twopence a quart. Porter, which was darker than the pale beers, became more popular, for a time.

About the same time beer was losing ground, in the cities particularly, to wine, which was increasingly popular, and to gin on which the poor could become drunk so cheaply. But by about 1790 the gin mania had largely subsided.

Pewter mugs were for the last few centuries commonly used in pubs, where they continued to serve until the end of the 19th century. By then they were valued and collected and thieving was rife. It is said that determined women were able to hide them under their long, full skirts and make away with them sometimes to the extent of having a circular row hung on hooks around their waists. Some pubs continued to secure them behind the bar, for special or regular customers, and even today some people have their private pots waiting for them behind the bar.

In America beer was vital for the passengers on the *Mayflower* and the founding of the colonies. It not only was a sanitary alternative to stagnant water aboard the pilgrim ships, but was recognized as having health-giving properties. The pilgrims even decided to land sooner than planned because, as a journal of the *Mayflower* voyage published in 1622 records '. . . we could not now take time for further search or consideration: our victuals being much spent, especially our beer.'[3] John Alden, whom Longfellow immortalized in *The Courtship of Miles Standish*

---

[3] 'Beer and Ale', *Collier's Encyclopedia*, Vol. 3, P. F. Collier & Son Corporation, pp. 283–286.

CHARLES WEST COPE. R.A. *Florence Cope at Dinnertime.* 23×27½ inches. Robin Carver, Esq.

Exhibited at the Royal Academy in 1852. Florence Cope was the artist's daughter. The silver mug is in the possession of a descendant of the artist.

Reproduced from *Victorian Painters* by Jeremy Maas (Barrie & Jenkins Ltd., 1970).

15

('Speak for yourself, John' said Priscilla when John was courting her on behalf of Standish), was hired in Southampton to be cooper for the pilgrim party.

Beer was first brewed commercially in the United States in New Amsterdam (later New York) in about 1633. Although it was imported, home brewing was much encouraged, and in 1789 the Massachusetts legislature passed an act exempting brewers from taxation for a five-year period saying, 'the wholesome qualities of malt liquors greatly recommend them to general use, as an important means of preserving the health of the citizens of this commonwealth.'[4] Samuel Adams, signer of the Declaration of Independence and called the 'Father of the American Revolution', was a Massachusetts brewer.

Many colonial Americans had their own brewhouses, such as William Penn who built one in Bucks County, Pennsylvania, in 1683. George Washington had his own private recipe.

The 1840s were a turning point for American beer, and a change-over took place from English beer to a German-type lager. The industry flourished during the 19th century and later until Prohibition in 1920. At that time draught beer comprised 79 percent of beer consumption, but after the end of prohibition in 1933 the style of drinking beer changed radically. Bottled or canned beer now constitutes the main form of beer consumption and most of it is consumed in the home. The use of the mug or tankard became totally obsolete in favour of drinking from the container itself or a glass, and, of course, American beer is drunk cold. In fact, the use of mugs and tankards probably ceased much earlier, soon after Louis Pasteur's discoveries in the 1870s made bottling commercially viable. With the development of the pressed glass technique from the 1820s at such firms as the Boston and Sandwich Glass Company, it was to be expected that Americans would use glass principally rather than pewter or silver, which were more expensive. However, the rare items of early silver and pewter tankards are much sought-after, and are more expensive than the more common English equivalents. As for 19th-century examples, these too have been gulped up by a thirsty American

[4] Ibid.

collecting public.

Pewter was indispensable to the Pilgrims. It was the common tableware up to the early 1800s. It is so scarce today because the demand from modern collectors far exceeds the relatively small quantity that was originally made to supply a comparatively tiny population.

No one could deny that drink has taken a fearful toll of human health and life and that it is capable of misuse – with the dire consequences illustrated in Hogarth's satirical engravings of 'Beer Street' and 'Gin Lane'. The ignorance that allowed beer to be taxed in order to encourage the drinking of spirits in the 18th century also led to the downfall of American settlers from the English West Country, who missed their jug of cider on the table and thought they had found an admirable substitute in whisky. Drunk on gin for a penny a time or insensate on a jug of cheap whisky! Is it any wonder that the temperance movement found ready converts in the 19th century!?

But, equally, no one could deny the pleasure drink has given through the ages, so much pleasure that writers and poets, doubtless sometimes inspired by the muse of alcohol, have immortalized their happy hours over a tankard of beer, a mug of ale or a cup of wine. Writers like Dr Samuel Johnson and Shakespeare have been propaganda masters for the pleasures of drink, while others such as C. S. Calverley (1831–1884) have made fun of the pleasure. Writes Calverley in 'Beer',

> O Beer! O Hodgson, Guinness, Allsop, Bass!
> Names that should be on every infant's tongue . . . .

> The heart which grief hath cankered
> Hath one unfailing remedy – The Tankard . . . .

> He that would shine, and petrify his tutor
> Should drink draught Allsop in its 'native pewter'.

But, jest apart, Dr Johnson, probably in all seriousness, is said to have commented that a tavern chair was the throne of human felicity.

Shakespeare's characters too spoke much about the joys of drinking ale. '. . . a quart of ale is a dish for a king' he says in 'The

Winter's Tale'. And in 'Henry VI', 'I will make it felony to drink small beer.'

It is difficult to present a clear picture of who was drinking from what, when, because during the centuries there have been a number of materials from which the drinker could choose. If I speak of the well-to-do Elizabethan drinking ale from a silver or gilt mug or tankard, it might be pointed out that he might well have preferred his ale in Venetian glasses. If I speak of lesser mortals using pewter, I may be contradicted and told they drank from stoneware pots. All one can say with any certainty is that human behaviour is inconsistent and contradictory and that collectors today have a varied selection of mugs and tankards to own as a result. However, the following is an attempt to paint a general picture of the evolution of the use of mugs and tankards.

There is in existence a mug *circa* 50 BC – 50 AD which is housed in the Merseyside County Museum. It is Celtic – made of yew wood, bronze and brass with a beautiful cast-bronze scrolled handle. The body is concave, $5\frac{9}{16}$ inches high and $7\frac{3}{16}$ inches in diameter.

In the Middle Ages the use of treen for tableware was virtually universal among those who could not afford silver and pewter. Wooden tankards were in common use in households and taverns. Wooden platters, dishes, bowls, goblets, beakers and spoons were also common until Tudor times when a more settled era allowed an improvement in standards, and caused pottery to take the place of treen for tableware.

The term 'tankard' may not have been used for the same vessel we know today as a tankard. We do know that large 'tanggard pots' of wood with covers and handles were in use in the Middle Ages to carry water from wells and conduits. Mugs or 'cans' as they were called were probably in use in the 15th century or earlier of wood, pewter and earthenware. Certainly from the next century we have references to cans and pots in these materials. A 16th-century drinking song begins 'Now God be with old Simeon, for he made cans for many a one.'[5] These were probably pewter mugs.

---

[5] *How to Identify English Silver Drinking Vessels*, Douglas Ash, G. Bell & Sons, Ltd.

A French priest, Etienne Perlin, who visited England in 1558, wrote, 'As to the way of life of the English, they are somewhat impolite, for they belch at the table without reserve or shame, even before persons of the greatest dignity. They consume great quantities of beer, double and single, and drink it, not out of glasses, but from earthen pots with handles and covers of silver, even in the houses of persons of medium wealth, and as for the poor, the covers of their pots are only of pewter, and in some villages their beer pots are made of wood.'[6] The handles, in fact, were probably of pottery overlaid with silver, and the 'pots' referred to were tankards.

Leather jacks which can be jugs, or mugs, are mentioned in Shakespeare's writings as used for wine or ale by aristocrats and plain shepherds alike.

Leather vessels may have been used from earliest times, when

[6] Quoted in *How to Identify English Silver Drinking Vessels,* Douglas Ash, G. Bell & Sons, Ltd.

The lovely bell-shape that appeared in various materials during the 18th century is seen here in Longton Hall porcelain circa 1758-60 with the added advantage of having a transfer-print of the Right Honourable William Pitt by J. Sadler, the man in the forefront of early mass-produced transfer-printed commemorative ware. *Photograph: Winifred Williams.*

primitive man accidentally dropped hot stones into leather bags used to carry water. As the bags cooled and dried, they hardened into shapes. They were made until the early 19th century, and many reproductions and fakes have appeared since. Basically, the shapes were created by impregnating the leather with cold water, draining the surplus off and moulding it into shape by hand, over formers or by using moulds, dies or presses.

Although wine, ale, beer and mead were drunk from the same vessels, the growing demand for tankards from the 16th century onwards coincided with the tendency for the two main camps to separate. By the second half of the 17th century the wine drinker with his glass or cup, and the beer drinker with his tankard or mug, tended to stick to their own drinks, viz a contemporary rhyme that goes,

Of honest malt and liquor let English boys sing;
A pox take French claret, we'll drink no such thing.

Of course, wine cups with handles would be at home in any collection of beer vessels. Certainly there were times when ale was as strong or stronger than wine and drunk from equally small vessels, such as the 18th-century 'ales' or ale glasses. Western writings are full of references to wine, from St Paul's saying 'Take a little wine for thy stomach's sake' and Noah getting drunk, through Chaucer, Shakespeare, Boswell, and *Tom Brown's Schooldays*. Sir Toby Belch is tippling from 'a stoop of wine' in 'Twelfth Night' as he chides Olivia's puritanical steward, Malvolio, 'Art any more than a steward? Dost thou think because thou art virtuous, there shall be no more cakes and ale?'

Strong ale in the late 17th century was drunk from glasses, as well as mugs and tankards, but small or weaker beer would definitely need large vessels, such as mugs of stoneware, pewter and jacked leather, and tankards of pewter and silver and, occasionally, wood. Production of silver tankards increased enormously in the reigns of Charles II, James II and William and Mary. Elizabethan silver tankards and those from the mid-17th century were mostly of about one pint capacity, but the well-known revellings of the Restoration may have increased the size of tankards to quart and even three-pint sizes. However, some of these, or, indeed, all of the large tankards may, as mentioned before, have been used as serving vessels.

The 18th century was the finest hour for mugs and tankards. People entertained each other at home, treating each other to ale, beer, porter and cider out of exquisitely made mugs and tankards of silver, glass, porcelain, pewter and pottery. The middle and upper classes doubtless preferred the more expensive silver, porcelain and glass, though many had to make do with pewter as a substitute for the first.

Pewter reigned supreme in the tavern during the 18th and 19th centuries, although glass rummers and stoneware pots were probably also used for ale. Glass was probably introduced gradually towards the end of the century when machines were used to mass-produce pressed glass.

Mugs and tankards were by no means for the exclusive use of alcoholic beverages. Mugs for children were made in all materials, particularly in the 19th century when christening mugs were popular.

The names of inns and public houses are a story in themselves. The earliest were for religious pilgrims with such names as the 'Star', the 'Mitre', and the 'Trip to Jerusalem' in Nottingham which is one of the oldest pubs in England, dating from about 1070 and originally called the 'Pilgrim'.

'The Green Man' apparently refers to woodsmen and, judging from this passage from a manuscript of about 1610, from the Harleian collection formed by Robert Harley (1661–1724) and his son Edward (1689–1741), Earls of Oxford, they were highly susceptible to strong drink:

> They are called woudmen or wildmen thou at thes days in ye signe call them Green Men, covered with grene boughs: and are used for signes by stillers of strong watters and if I mistake not are yet supporters of ye King of Denmarks armes at thes day; and I am apt to believe that ye Daynes learned us hear in England the use of those intosticating licker which berefts them of their sences.

I doubt if the Danes were entirely to blame for the English woodsmen's love of 'intosticating licker'.

Many other pub signs represented the trades that frequented them, such as 'Jolly Blacksmith' and 'Painter's Arms'.

Chapter Two
SILVER

An incalculable amount of silver has been lost to posterity through voluntary liquidation by its owners, either for coinage or to be fashioned into new styles, perhaps because it had worn out through use. However, what survives is still considerable and is preciously treated by present-day owners: even though ownership changes somewhat too frequently due to industrious thieving!

Mugs and tankards and other drinking vessels have been the most important portion of the silversmith's output throughout time, from the silver-rimmed drinking horns of the Saxons to the presentation mugs so popular as gifts today.

It is generally agreed today that a mug is a vessel of approximately pint or half-pint size with a handle and no lid, while a tankard has a lid. A flagon is a form of large tankard. However, these vessels have frequently overlapped in function and definition. Silver tankards in particular have been made in many sizes and could be used to serve the ale into smaller mugs or tankards of silver, pewter, pottery or whatever.

The term 'tankard' stems from the Middle Ages when it referred to a large wooden pot with a handle and cover for carrying water. Pewter 'tanggard pots' were in use in 1482, but the use of the term 'silver tankard' appears about the mid-16th century. Some 'pots' of silver of varying sizes, for serving and drinking, were in use from the Middle Ages and were probably similar to our concept of mugs and tankards today; however, most pots would have been of pottery, wood or pewter.

Up to and including the Tudor period, mazers, beakers and horns were the main silver or silver-mounted vessels used by the better off for wine, ale and mead.

The earliest type of silver tankard in existence is pot-bellied

with a short cylindrical neck, flared rim and large foot-ring. The handle is curved and joined in two places, much as it is, with slight variations, on all types of mugs and tankards. The lid is a flattened dome resting on a flanged edge to which the handle and hinge are attached. Based on an ancient form of pottery vessel, it was made by raising from a flat sheet of silver.

There were also vessels made of glass, horn, marble, Chinese porcelain and salt glazed stoneware and mounted in silver. Most common were the Rhineland stoneware tankards which looked magnificent combined with the silver, and many more have survived than the solid silver tankards of the period. The quotation cited in the introduction about the English consuming great quantities of beer 'not out of glasses, but from earthenware pots with handles and lids of silver' would seem to refer to this Elizabethan type of drinking vessel.

The rich of the second half of the 16th century were drinking from silver-gilt vessels either of a tall cylindrical flagon type with lids customarily of a domed variety, or a shorter, wider tankard tapering slightly inward at the top. Both were likely to be well-ornamented in Elizabethan style. James I (1603–1625) tankards were generally plainer and not usually gilded.

An interesting and short-lived vessel appeared under Charles I (1625–1649), which lacked a foot-ring so important to prevent

Left: Charles II cylindrical silver tankard with beaded handle, thumbpiece of entwined dolphins, and acanthus leaf embossing. It is engraved with the arms of the Worshipful Company of Goldsmiths. Maker GS 1681 *Photograph: Christie's*

Right: Charles II York silver tankard of the Scandinavian type which sometimes had pins or pegs on the inside for measuring ones draught when drinking in fellowship. To "drink a merry pin" or take someone "down a peg" derives from these and ordinary British peg tankards. This was by M. Best, 1670. Pomegranate feet with leaves above are characteristic of this relatively rare type of tankard. Lids usually had no projecting flanges and the handles were often double-scrolls. *Photograph: N. Bloom and Son Ltd.*

23

Charles II three-pint silver tankard, London 1683.

Miniature James II silver tankard by George Mainjoy, 1686, with double-stepped lid and acanthus leaf embossing characteristic of the late 17th century. Silver "toys" like the tankard (and punch bowl beside it) have always been great favourites with the elite and this was no exception having sold for £550.
Photograph: Christie's

wearing out the bottom of the tankard. At the same time, the vessel became wider. The foot-ring was restored to greater prominence than ever in the 1640s, in the form of a skirt-base that not only protected the tankard from springing leaks but gave it great stability – useful for table-pounding pub debates between Royalists and Roundheads.

A low, flat-topped dome appeared just before the Commonwealth period and became known as 'single-stepped' in contrast to the 'double-stepped' lids that came in during the lavish times of

Charles II. Much silver was, of course, melted down and converted into coin to pay for both armies, which is why little survives from the period prior to the Restoration. Even Charles II had his men drinking from pewter while times were rough.

However, once restored to power, the Merry Monarch was the inspiration behind the lavish use of silver. Whereas during Elizabethan times and up to the Restoration in 1660 the pint capacity was usual, the well-to-do populace suddenly developed a tremendous thirst, and quart or more capacities were usual in silver tankards. At the same time, however, mugs, or 'cans' as they were called, remained pint-sized, which rather lends weight to Mr Arthur Binsted's thesis that the tankards were used to serve the beer into mugs. Probably both theories are correct: that the large tankards could be used by gluttons, as well as for serving. Certainly the restoration of the silversmithing craft to high status encouraged smiths to want to lavish attention and metal on large vessels. Also, tankards were used for serving sack or spiced wine, and pegged tankards were used for drinking in fellowship. Pegs are rarely found on silver tankards made after the early part of the 18th century.

Left: Extremely rare Gateshead silver tankard by Augustin Float, circa 1690. Float served his apprenticeship in London but preferred to return to his native Gateshead to produce his magnificent work. *Photograph: Christie's*

Right: A James II silver mug by EG, 1686, with S-shaped handle of thin sheet silver characteristic of this style. The globular shape of the body with its short cylindrical neck is clearly derived from earlier pottery forms.

25

William and Mary bulbous silver tankard engraved with a coat of arms within a foliate and scrolled cartouche and decorated at the base with cut card work. The flat domed cover has a similar cut card decoration and sphere finial. S-scroll handle with large hinge, scrolled billet and shield-shaped finial, 6½ inches high.
Photograph: Henry Spencer & Sons

During the Restoration Period tankards are recognizable by their wide cylindrical girth in relation to height. There are a number of plain examples surviving in both silver and pewter. But various kinds of decorative motifs were also common. The so-called 'cut-card' technique was used in Charles II tankards, but became even more popular under the Huguenot silversmiths in the reign of Queen Anne (1702–1714). The technique consisted of cutting shapes such as leaf forms from sheet metal and soldering them to the body of the tankard. Another type of attractive decoration was Dutch-influenced and consisted of acanthus leaves and plainer palmette leaves embossed on the lower part of the body and sometimes on the lid. A third type of decoration was a naive kind of chinoiserie design chased or engraved on the body, such as trees, birds and Oriental figures.

At this time both single and double-stepped lids were made, although the upper step was still narrow compared with its development in later years.

When the Huguenot refugees from religious persecution in Europe arrived on the English scene after the repeal of the Edict of Nantes in 1685, they were to have a great influence on English silversmithing. They distinguished themselves early on by their standards of decoration and form and generous use of the precious metal. They were noted for tasteful fluting and gadrooning and cable-moulding and applied cut-card work.

Although doubtless made before, the earliest surviving silver mugs are from the Charles II period. They are a bulbous pottery form with short necks and handles of thin sheet silver. The typical cylindrical form tapering slightly at the top edge, that become so familiar in both silver and pewter, appeared in the 1680s with a more substantial D-shaped handle, hollow but of heavy silver. For further comfort it had a thumb rest at the top of the handle.

The making of silver mugs increased during the latter half of the 17th century and early part of the 18th, with a decline in the production of tankards partly due to the introduction of the higher Britannia standard in 1696 and hence the increasing cost of silver. At the same time, drinking wine from silver vessels became less fashionable, with the advancement of the lead glass industry.

By the time of Queen Anne there were both mugs and tankards of baluster shape, but these did not become popular until later in the century. In the second half of the 18th century they were more common than cylindrical types. An odd baluster mug was made

Left: George I silver tankard with domed cover becoming popular at this time

Right: George I silver mug by Thomas Mason 1722. The shape is a cross between the cylindrical and baluster mugs.

George II silver baluster mug with scroll handle, 1728, maker T.E.

Left: George II plain baluster silver tankard with scroll handle, openwork thumbpiece and domed cover, 8¼ inches high, London 1755.

Right: George III silver tankard by Whiplam and Wright, London, 1761. Photograph: Riddett and Adams Smith

for a short time with more-or-less straight sides that 'tucked-in' just above the foot-ring. The more curvaceous baluster mugs popular in the latter part of the century usually had cast single or double scroll handles.

In about 1700 domes began to appear on tankard lids which had heretofore been flat. These domes continued throughout the century and into the 19th, although a type of flat-lidded tankard was also popular. The dome accompanied the increasingly slender

trend of the cylindrical and baluster shapes very much associated with the Georgians.

A design which had first been seen in the middle of the century became popular for both mugs and tankards towards the end of the 18th century. It was reminiscent of a barrel with its wooden staves and hoops, or of early Scandinavian vessels made with binding bands of willow. Tankards were either cylindrical or barrel-shaped and were characterised by bands of horizontal reeding representing barrel hoops, and sometimes of vertical lines suggestive of staves. Lids were flat and handles frequently squared. Mug versions were usually half-pint size or smaller. Both continued to be made into the next century when, during the Regency period, the practical use of silver for beer-drinking declined, remaining in vogue largely for presentations, gifts and children's mugs. Tankards are virtually nonexistent after 1810, except for highly decorative ones intended for presentation, and modern ones.

Throughout most of the 18th century it was common for silversmiths to make a horizontal moulded band around the body of the tankard or mug, which was practical as well as decorative because it acted as a 'bumper' against denting. This feature also sometimes appeared earlier, in the 17th century, and often on pewter too.

Children's mugs of the 19th century, often given as christening presents, can be extremely attractive and are charming additions

Left: George III silver quart mug of baluster shape, scroll handle and typical moulded band encircling the widest part.

Right: George III silver tankards made in London by John Kidder in 1778 (left) and John Schofield (right). The straight-sided, cylindrical tankards such as these were less popular than baluster shapes at this time. *Photograph: Messenger May Baverstock*

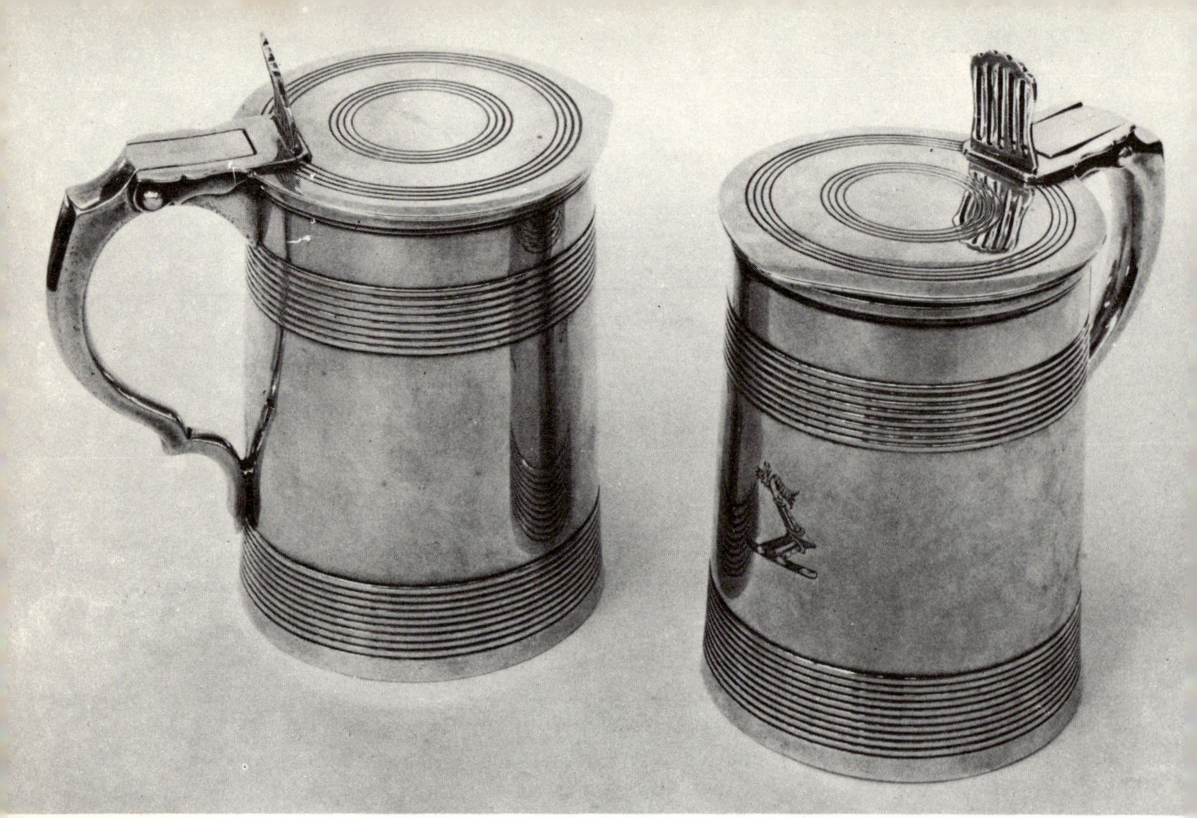

George III barrel-type silver tankards with glass bases and flat lids, 5¾ inches high, 1802. The horizontal ribbing is reminiscent of barrel hoops. *Photograph: King and Chasemore*

to a collection. They are not necessarily very expensive either.

Other Victorian mugs were made under the influence of Art Nouveau design, with the characteristic tendril shapes, and they often incorporate medieval ideas by the use of rivets, for instance, and the imitation of a wrought-iron look.

Recent years have seen the most important crafts revival for 50 years or more. English silver crafts are widely sought at home

Below: Left to right: George III straight sided silver mug decorated with two reeded bands, London 1810. A Russian silver mug decorated with repousse peasant figures, circa 1879, 3½ inches high and a George II baluster silver mug with scroll handle, London 1743 by William Williams. *Photograph: King and Chasemore*

Victorian silver children's mugs of quarter to half-pint size. *Photograph: N. Bloom and Sons Ltd.*

and abroad. Designers such as Alex Styles, Gerald Benney and Stuart Devlin have become the Paul de Lameries (working 1712–1749) and Paul Storrs (working about 1792–1838) of the present. Mugs and tankards are made primarily to give as gifts or as commemorative collectors' pieces, but no doubt many a keen drinker of beer enjoys using antique or modern vessels in the privacy and protection of his home.

The term 'flagon' seems to have been first applied in the early 17th century, when instead of 'livery pot' the word 'flagon' was applied to a tall tankard used for drinking and serving. Many had an ecclesiastical use.

Early English flagons were larger versions of tankards. They might be of the bulbous-body type with short cylindrical necks and low-domed lids; or, more usually, straight-sided cylindrical with spreading base and domed lid with a knob; or of a tapering cylindrical body.

A movement towards simplicity in the early part of the 17th century reached its zenith during the Puritan Commonwealth era, continued to some degree even during the lavish days of Charles II, and returned again in force in the Queen Anne style.

American mugs and tankards are very similar to their English counterparts, and the earliest surviving ones date from the late 17th century just as do most of what is available in English vessels. The first American goldsmith, Robert Sanderson (1608–1693), was London-trained. Dutch-American silversmiths turned their hands to the English type of tankard, imparting to it greater elaboration in the handle and base moulding and sometimes on the cover too, thus establishing a distinctively 'American' style, or rather a New York style, for it was in New York that the Dutch lived. New England styles remained characteristically English, while Philadelphia tankards in the mid-18th century were large and sometimes curved. During the 18th century mugs and tankards were extremely popular with the entire populace. However, early in the 19th century the first effects of the temperance campaigns were to be seen in the conversion of many tankards into jugs by the addition of spouts.

Obviously, mugs and tankards were far more popular in Britain, America, Germany, Holland and Scandinavia than in France, Italy, Spain and Portugal, which are traditionally

Victorian child's silver mug with heavy embossing showing a bold, clearly defined design. It is of pint capacity, a rarity, as children's mugs are usually smaller. *Photograph: N. Bloom and Sons Ltd.*

The ancient craft of silversmithing is still very much alive today, in both traditional and modern guises. The latter is well-represented in these very modern mugs by Alex Styles.

The Styles mugs were presented by Flowers Brewery Ltd. to the County Borough of Luton. Styles is designer for Garrard, the famous jewellers.

wine-drinking areas. Germany, in particular, is noted for its love of beer and its large and elaborate tankards. Makers there had a fondness for using exotic materials for tankards and mugs, and mounting them with silver and silver-gilt: they used such materials as amber, Venetian latticinio glass, ostrich eggs, semi-precious stones, coconuts and Turkish pottery. Germany exported to England the mottled saltglaze stoneware 'tigerware' mentioned in the beginning of this chapter, which was mounted with silver during Elizabethan times. English makers too used some of these exotic materials, but to a far lesser extent than in Germany.

The techniques of fashioning silver have changed surprisingly

One of the key figures in the revival of silversmithing as a craft is Gerald Benney. His work is distinguished by a hand-texturing seen in these mugs. This is achieved by the use of a hammer which has a grooved surface and is applied with considerable force to the soft silver, leaving its impression. These textured surfaces were inspired by the fact that people were seen to handle new silver with too much respect, being afraid to leave fingermarks. The surface also inhibits tarnishing. The mugs are raised from one piece and not, therefore, soldered except at the handle. The inside surfaces are silver-gilt, and there is a plain silver rim around the drinking edge. The one with the small handle is a child's christening mug.

little over the centuries and much is still hand-made. Either the mug or tankard is raised from one piece by meticulously hammering it into shape, or already rolled sheets are soldered together. Obviously, collectors of the finest silver prefer the former method. Smaller parts such as handles and finials are often cast.

The main methods of decoration are chasing, embossing and engraving. In chasing, a kind of punch with a blunt end was struck with a hammer as it moved along, producing designs by compressing the metal. Embossing is done from the inside of the vessel, leaving a raised ornament on the outside. Engraving actually cuts furrows in the metal on the outside.

We owe a great debt to the tradition of English silversmithing for having established a hallmarking system from 1300, enabling us to date with accuracy not only silver styles, but pewter, glass and porcelain which, on the whole, shared similar styles.

English silver has also been keenly collected for the reasons that the quality and content of the silver are high, and that it can be melted down into coinage, if need be, in times of stress and war. During the Restoration on the other hand the reverse happened. The rich were so keen to have articles of silver that the coinage was melted down to make vessels, until a law was passed to overcome an acute financial crisis resulting from the practice. And in Tudor days the rich preferred to keep articles of silver rather than coins, following the debasement of the coinage by Henry VIII. The sterling silver mark is the lion passant (since about 1545), except in Scotland since 1758 where the thistle has been used, and Ireland where the sterling mark is the crowned harp. These marks denote 92·5 percent pure silver. The Britannia standard required between 1697 and 1720, and occasionally used since, is represented by the figure of Britannia which indicated

American silver tankard by Jacob Hurd of Boston, Massachusetts, circa 1735, with domed lid and typical moulded band around the body.
Photograph: Phillips

a higher silver content than the sterling standard.

Learning silver marks is like practising a new language and is equally rewarding, for it enables one to identify the date, maker and area at a glance and thus to evaluate if styles and hallmarks match. Edward I (1272–1307) established in 1300, by statute, the first mark, a crowned leopard's head (called the 'King's Mark'). The crown was removed in 1821 and the head has remained crownless ever since. A second mark, the maker's mark, which originated in 1363, was represented by signs or symbols or, later, by one or more of his initials. In 1739 it was required by law that the initials consist of first and surname only.

The date mark was required from about 1478. The letters 'a' to 'u' (except 'j') denote the years, with the style of the letters changing every twenty years. The shield enclosing the letters is also sometimes varied.

Although silversmithing has maintained a high standard in Britain, where punishments are laid down for those who would alter pieces or fake hallmarks, nevertheless fakes and alterations have occurred. More often and quite legitimately, pieces have been altered by repairs. With a commodity such as silver which is precious, not only for itself but for its place in the nation's heritage, it is as well to buy good, unrepaired examples.

Look for signs of solder or a yellowish cast to the silver. Breathing on a spot of a suspected repair may reveal differences in the metal. Soft solder indicates an inadequate repair and should be avoided: it is mainly lead and shows as a dull grey colour. Embossed articles are particularly vulnerable because the act of polishing can wear through the high relief. The silver is thinner and most stretched in these places anyway.

Unfortunately, though silver has been valued and cherished and greatly sought after throughout time, people generally have not liked to adopt silver tankards bearing the names or armorials of other people. They like to wipe these markings out and pretend they never existed. I don't know why. But most tankards had initials and coats of arms on them originally and many have been removed, leaving the vessels thin in these places. Personally, I think it is a shame to destroy the originality of a piece, and armorials and names add to its history. Besides thinness or a different colour or surface appearance, look for repairs which, even though prettily disguised by decorative engraving or embossing, affect the value. One should examine handles, feet and bottoms, which have borne most of the wear, as well as take care to look inside where repairs and alterations may show up most clearly. Embossing is suspect if it appears on a mug or tankard which was made when such decoration was out of fashion. Most vessels are hallmarked near the handle, but those marked underneath the handle should be examined carefully in case the handle was at some time moved to disguise a weak spot.

Another practice has been to change flat tankard covers to dome shapes and vice versa, depending on fashion. This causes stretching when converting from flat to domed; and an extra amount of metal when converting from domed to flat, resulting, perhaps, in a higher than usual flat lid.

Silver-gilt tankard made in Augsburg circa 1720.

Silver mugs are nearly always of pint capacity or less, and anything larger without a cover undoubtedly had one in the first place. Those with the lion thumbpiece are highly desirable. These were made towards the end of Charles II's reign and were popular in the early 18th century. But this thumbpiece should be regarded with suspicion if it appears on later tankards, for it may have been faked in an attempt to add to the value.

Large German parcel-gilt cylindrical flagon on spreading foot, elaborately chased with a stag, hounds and birds in scrollwork panels. with applied lion's masks, winged cherubs and rich engraving, circa 1580, probably Lubeck or Konigsberg. *Photograph: Christie's*

Chapter Three
PEWTER

No other material has suited the mug and tankard quite so admirably as pewter. On both utilitarian and aesthetic grounds, the shapes of the vessels and the substance of the metal have made a perfect marriage. Some devotees of the drink and the metal go so far as to maintain that beer tastes better in pewter.

Pewter has served the British Isles from Roman days and is still a perennial favourite with beer-drinkers. A collector of pewter vessels has the opportunity not only of living with its mellow colour and texture, but of observing national styles throughout the many countries where pewter has been used. The man known as the Dean of English Pewter, H. H. Cotterell, has written of the appeal of pewter 'which speaks to us "of our ain fireside" and weaves into the flickering lights of blazing logs, memories of our ancestors and days long since gone by.'[1]

The strength of form of pewter mugs and tankards suits their utilitarian – not to mention enjoyable – purpose of containing the drink of hardy men. Not for ceramics, glass or silver the test of being banged on the strong oak table in order to emphasize a point. (Mind you, this practice has accounted for the loss of countless of these vessels to posterity, for constant denting caused them to be melted down and made into new styles).

Along with pottery, leather and wood, pewter is one of the oldest materials to be widely used for drinking vessels. It enjoyed a high point during the 17th century, but has been important throughout much of British history.

No pewter mugs or tankards exist from earlier than the 16th

---

[1] *National Types of Old Pewter*, Howard Hershel Cotterell, Adolphe Riff and Robert M. Vetter, Revised and Expanded Edition, The Pyne Press, Princeton, 1972. Originally published in the magazine *Antiques*.

William III flat-lidded tankard with ram's horn thumbpiece and denticulation at front; the body or drum engraved in wriggled work (a flat-ended tool is pivoted on its edges) with half-length portrait of King William III in a roundel and conventional floral motifs; inscribed "God blefs K. William"; indecipherable touch mark in base, circa 1695. Overall height 6½ inches.
Photograph: Worshipful Company of Pewterers

century, but pewter drinking vessels were in use in Roman times and then re-introduced into Britain in about the 14th or 15th century. The Anglo-Saxons and those living under Norman and Plantagenet rule used wood, leather and horn, and when pewter was introduced again, only the top people could afford it.

In about 1500, pewter was too expensive to be common and there are records showing that Henry VIII took steps to prevent his pewter from being stolen. Only late in the 16th and early in the 17th centuries did pewter begin to be more widely owned. At this time household inventories mention 'pewter pots', 'pewter flagons' and 'pewter flagon pots'.[2]

About 1587 William Harrison wrote in his *Description of England* 'As for drinks, it is usuallie filled in pots, gobblets, jugs, bols of silver in noblemens houses, also in fine Venice glasses of all formes, and for want of these, elsewhere, in pots of earth sundrie colours and moulds, whereof manie are garnished with silver, or at the leastwise in pewter.'[3] Many pots, goblets, jugs and bowls of this time were pewter. As for the pots garnished with pewter, these were an important part of the pewterer's trade from the 14th century. These 'pots' were what we now call mugs and tankards and were the pot-bellied stoneware vessels imported from the German Rhineland. It is recorded that in France there were quart and pint tankards in use in the 16th century, and an English source of 1612–1613 mentions 'quarts and pints with or without lids.'[4]

While in the 14th and 15th centuries one might drink from pottery, leather, pewter, wood or horn, it was possibly pewter

---

[2] *The Pewter Collector* by H. J. L. J. Massé, revised with additions by Ronald F. Michaelis Barrie and Jenkins, 1971, p. 67.
[3] Ibid, p. 76.
[4] Ibid, p. 77.

Flat-lidded pewter tankard of the William and Mary period decorated in wriggled work with a crown and the inscription "God Bless King William." The thumbpiece in the shape of a crown is unique. *Photograph: R. Mundey*

Left: William and Mary pewter tankard with flat lid, serrated projecting flange, and engraved ("Wriggled" by means of a flat-ended tool pivoted on its edges) portraits on the drum, c. 1690.
Right: Charles II pewter tankard with wriggled engraving, c. 1680. Mundey Collection.

that first provided a reliable measure to ensure that the customer had received what he had paid for. Alehouses must have been notoriously lax on this score, for in 1423 Robert Chichely, Lord Mayor of London, made a regulation 'That retailers of ale should sell the same in their houses in pots of "peutre" sealed and open, and that whoever carried ale to the buyer should hold the pot in one hand and a cup in the other; and that all who had pots unsealed should be fined.'[5]

Even earlier, William the Conqueror ordained that 'measures and weights should be true and stamped in all parts of the Kingdom', and the practice of stamping measures as a guarantee of accuracy seems to have been inaugurated in the reign of Edward I (1272–1307) who ordained that 'no measure shall be in any town unless it do agree with the King's measure.'[6]

Various sovereigns from the time at least of Henry VII required the stamping of a seal on pewter to conform to varying standards,

---

[5] Ibid, p. 75.
[6] 'A Pewter Hammerhead Baluster Measure of circa 1530', Roland J. A. Shelley, *Apollo*, June 1974, pp. 156–7.

and in 1826 the Imperial measure came into force. Vessels used in drinking establishments were required to bear seals testifying to the fact that they conformed to the Imperial measure. This was 20 fluid ounces per pint, which was very close to the old Ale Standard.

Pewter is, broadly speaking, tin mixed with varying quantities of brass, copper, lead, antimony or bismuth.

Pewterers were divided into specialisations, e.g. makers of flat-ware, such as plates and chargers, makers of hollow-ware, such as flagons, tankards, pots, jugs and mugs, spoon-makers, etc. Tankards and flagons were cast in several pieces and soldered or fused together: the seams can be detected on the bodies of vessels. The handles were often hollow cast by pouring the hot metal into a mould, then when the metal next to the mould cooled, the mould was reversed and the unset inner metal allowed to flow out again. The resulting rough castings would be finished by hammering, and on the lathe.

Pewter-making standards in Britain were very much regulated

Left: A rare late 17th century pewter mug (often called "tavern pots"), the cylindrical drum with two bands, c. 1695.
Right: William III drinking mug, 1690.
Back: Broad-rim pewter plate, c. 1660-80. Mundey collection.

by the Guild (the charter for the founding of the Pewterers Company was granted in 1473) and English pewter gained a worldwide reputation.

There is some misunderstanding about the nature of Britannia metal. It is definitely pewter, but contains almost entirely tin and antimony and no lead at all. It first appeared about 1770, but not much was made commercially until seven to ten years later. Britannia metal sometimes looks cold, hard and new, compared with the softer, mellower pewter containing lead and most objects were shaped by spinning, a cheaper method than casting. Before it dropped out of use in the 1860s, it was made by such firms as Dixon and Sons, Dixon and Smith, Broadhead and Atkin, I. Vickers, Wolstenholme, Ashberry, Colsman's Improved Compost, Stacey, Holesworth, and Smith, Kirkby and Co., whose names very often are stamped on Britannia ware.

English pewter was recognised as superior even by the Continentals, evidenced by the fact that they sometimes struck

Right: James I pewter flagon circa 1610, 13½ inches high. This is the earliest type of English flagon seen. *Photograph: Phillips*

Left: Early 18th century English baluster measure, pint capacity of the Old English Wine Standard, with a "bud" thumbpiece, circa 1700-1740. *Photograph: R. Mundey*

Rare George II pewter mug with heart-shaped terminal to the handle, 1750. Pewter mugs were used not only in taverns but given as christening presents, as were small silver mugs. Photograph: R. Mundey

'London' on their wares and 'English tin', referring to pewter made in the English manner. Great Britain and the Netherlands were noted for undecorated wares, relying upon the strength of form and the quality of the metal to stand alone. However there is no justification for too much snobbery in this respect, for the more decorated Continental wares are increasingly appreciated by British collectors. Moreover, although pewter was used for many centuries before, collectable pewter is only about 200 years old, and the diminishing amount left does not allow one to be unreasonably choosey.

While, during the 17th and 18th centuries, pewter and silver were rivals and were made into mugs and tankards of similar styles, the inspiration for their earlier vessels came from wooden, bronze and pottery shapes. Even the Continental heart-shaped tankard and flagon lid could be attributed to the basic ceramic pot with its pinched spout. The Austrian 'Stitzen' flagon is derived from a similar shape in treen built from wooden staves. And the same can be said about the type of mug and tankard with horizontal reeding around the body or drum, which on treen were binding bands of willow.

In the 16th and 17th centuries, pewter was much used for the important task of containing and serving the liquid, and the drink-

A display of pewter drinking, serving and measuring vessels showing relative sizes. Left to right: 18th century Swiss flagon, Scottish 19th century pear-shaped measure of one-half gallon capacity, William and Mary tankard, circa 1690, with maker's mark IB, a flat-lidded flagon, circa 1690 and an 18th century Swiss flagon from Berne with characteristic long spout. Shown with Charles II pewter Communion charger. *Photograph: Sotheby's*

ing vessels were not only of pewter but of pottery, leather, silver, wood and glass.

The other principal function of pewter vessels was to measure the liquid out to recipients. The earliest English measures are probably the 'wedge' type of baluster, the name resulting from the wedge shape of the piece connecting the lid with the handle. The baluster shape was the most customary for measures until well into the 18th century.

Although few collectors will be able now to lay their hands on 17th-century English pewter without colossal expense, this is considered to have been the heyday in this field. Pewter mugs were made from the late 17th century to *c.* 1720 in tapering cylindrical form, decorated, if at all, with a band of gadrooning, moulded base and mouldings or reeds around the body. They are less squat than the conventional Stuart tankard. Some were marked with names of the tavern and often of the innkeeper and the date, as well as a seal to verify capacity. This was a practice continued during the 18th century and well into the 19th century, doubtless as a practical means of keeping tabs on stock as pubs do with their glasses today.

Pewter mugs were standard for use in drinking establishments until the late 19th century and into the beginning of the 20th, although in the home they had long-since been displaced by porcelain, glass and fine earthenware (after having in their turn, ousted coarse earthenware and treen). They were also loaned out for the evening to customers. An American who lived with a family in London wrote in 1796 that the family sent out to any one of numerous tap-houses for a pint or quart of ale and that . . .

Some tulip-shaped pewter tankards c. 1760-1780 with a West Country one-half gallon wine measure c. 1800 on the right, which has a similarity to the Irish "haystack" measure, and an oval meat dish c. 1770 in the back. *Photograph: R. Mundey*

... the tap-house man ... sends his servant with it to your house, and also provides mugs for the purpose. They are always made of pewter, and have the owner's name engraved on the side. Every morning the servants from the tap houses go round and gather in their mugs which they string on a leather strap and carry on their shoulders home.[7]

Most mug collectors will have to content themselves with examples of pewter mugs from the late 18th century and the 19th. From about 1715 onwards most cylindrical mugs and tankards carry a single fillet moulding around the drum at some point. Mugs made from about 1720 to the late 18th century tend to follow tankard styles, particularly the tulip shape and a type in which the drum curves inwards just above the foot-ring, sometimes referred to as a 'bell'. In silver a similar shape is known as 'tucked in'. The glass-bottomed mug or tankard first appeared in the 1820s in pewter and is said to have enabled one to see enemies approaching while drinking.

Pewterers were anxious to keep abreast of rapidly changing fashions in silverware mainly because their customers required it. New pewter looked very like silver and anyone who could not afford a tankard of silver could request a similar one to be made in pewter. Silver was used by nobles but pewter was also used by them when they did not want, for one reason or another, to bring out the silver.

[7] *British Pewter*, Ronald F. Michaelis Ward Lock & Co., p. 21.

Below, left: Two 18th century Scottish 10 inch high flagons, the left hand example stamped with the maker's touch mark inside the base of a sailing ship with the words "S. Maxwell Success to Y. British Colonies." Stephen Maxwell of Glasgow is mentioned in 1781 as a copper and white-ironsmith of Maxwell Street and in 1784 as a pewterer. The right-hand example is engraved "High Meeting House Berwick 1774." Touch mark inside base is William Hunter of Edinburgh. In 1773 he had his shop in West Bow Street. *Photograph: Christopher Sykes Antiques*

Right: The distinction between flagons and large tankards is not an absolute one. Tankards were sometimes used to serve and flagons to drink from. In any case the "Tappit-Hen" like this one is a favourite with pewter collectors. The term refers specifically to this type of Scottish pewter measure. This one is late 18th century and holds three English pints. The owners initials A.C. are on the rim and like most Tappit-Hens does not have a maker's touch mark on it. *Photograph: Christopher Sykes Antiques.*

Handles of the 17th century could be solid straps of metal or they could be hollow cast. They were generously curved, with a piece that extended beyond the point of attachment and ended in what resembled a fish tail, a shield or a ball. In the late 18th century handles were of various types: similar to the hollow-cast ones with extended terminals mentioned above, fixed flat to the drum with no extension, double-curved and other forms. After the Imperial measure was introduced in 1826 measures and mugs sometimes were hard to separate as certain ones were used interchangeably. The bellied shape was, however, clearly only to be used as a measure.

The single fillet moulding became wider and more ornamental from the late 18th century. Those with fish-tail finials or ball finials probably developed from the lidded tankard. There were concave mugs of the 19th century principally made from about 1826 and later. The in-curved cylindrical mug on a foot-ring, usually with a scrolled or later squared handle, was popular

Scottish Tappit-Hen measure of 18th century Aberdeen type, made without a lid but still having a hinge lug unslotted for a hinge. *Photograph: Christopher Sykes Antiques*

during the 19th century.

From the 17th century, there are far fewer surviving mugs than tankards, mainly because fewer were made. But tankards, too, are scarce. Usually, the earliest examples one sees on the market, and then only infrequently, are the beautiful Stuart and William and Mary tankards of squarish proportions, with flat or domed lids with extended serrated brims in the front. The drums are plain or decorated in 'wriggled work'[8] engraving of portraits, flowers, birds and other subjects. The top end of the handle is soldered to the body and is capped by a lovely thumbpiece, such as the 'ram's horn', 'lovebirds', a variety of scrolls, etc.

The dome cover began to appear on pewter tankards during the last quarter of the 17th century, and in the 18th century it completely superseded the flat lid, though the shaped ornamental

[8] A flat-ended tool is 'wriggled' along, pivoting on its edges.

projections at the front of the cover survived for a short while. While the Stuart tankards had plain drums or were decorated with wriggled work engraving, the later domed-lid tankards carried the single fillet moulding around the drum, a feature carried on in mugs into the 19th century. The 'ramshorn' thumbpiece of the Stuart tankard evolved into a taller 'scroll' thumbpiece and later into the 'chairback'.

The dome-lidded tankard lasted from about 1680–1780 or so, and was usually short and squat with a slight tapering towards the top. There were also the slightly curved 'tulip' shapes made, but these are rarer. The latter shape was carried on in mugs after the lidded variety ceased to be made. By about 1770 the position of mugs and tankards was reversed, with more mugs than tankards being produced. But examples of both from the late 18th and 19th centuries can be difficult to date, as many of the 18th-century styles were carried into the next century.

Very often mugs and tankards are found signed by more than one maker. No one knows exactly why this occurred, but one might presume that they shared premises and would help each other out by lending castings or half-finished items to each other when an order had to be filled quickly.

Late 18th century barrel-shaped pewter mug, double-banded with scrolled or "broken" handle. These were made in quart, pint and half-pint sizes from the late 18th century to the early 19th and were also made in other materials such as silver and pottery.

Conventional pre-Victorian pint tavern mugs with single fillet moulding around the drum. The one on the left is circa 1820 and on the right circa 1775. The disc of metal seen at the top attachment of the handle of the right-hand mug was used for strengthening during the last 25 years of the 18th century but disappeared later. The shape of these mugs is squatter than earlier examples and the handles stop abruptly at the base without the earlier type of extension. *Photograph: R. Mundey*

The earliest known English flagons were cylindrical with nicely proportioned domed covers and skirts around the base, but sans the engraving often found on contemporary Continental examples. A similar English flagon, but later, has a longer skirt, a more substantial and flatter dome and a wider sweep of the handle and a massive thumbpiece.

Dutch paintings of the 17th and 18th centuries, such as those by Jan Steen, show in use the long-spouted flagons now named after the artist, stoneware pots with pewter lids and drinking glasses. The former seem largely to be for serving, although one Steen painting, 'Happy Family', shows a young child drinking from one.

In Scotland appeared the pot-bellied type of flagon, similar to the earlier Jan Steen, but without the long spout. In Holland we see a similar type without the spout and with the 'twin-ball' thumbpiece.

The 18th century provided the collector with many fine flagons and measures, such as the archetype of a pewter vessel, the famous

An example of the much-maligned and mis-interpreted Britannia metal is this mug by James Dixon and Son, circa 1830-33, which looks like any other pewter and in fact is. The difference between Britannia metal and other pewter is that the former is a type of pewter which contains no lead and rather more antimony which is a hardening agent. But all pewter is basically tin. Britannia metal lent itself to being worked much thinner than cast pewter and was thus employed in the more efficient and cheaper method of making spun pewter, an industrial advancement that caused the decline of the traditional cast pewter. However, this mug is an exception, and a vital lesson for the collector, for it was cast and made from Britannia metal. *Photograph: R. Mundey*

Scottish Tappit-Hen measure. The name is, speaking technically, applied incorrectly, because originally it referred only to a type of measure with a capacity of three pints. The same shape in smaller sizes were the 'chopine' and the 'mutchkin', but all were shaped like the tappit-hen. The name is now applied to all sizes of this shape.

English baluster measures are another type of pewter vessel, which appeals to mug and tankard collectors. They were made for wine and spirits, in capacities based on the Old English Wine Measure which is five-sixths of the Imperial standard measure that came into force in 1826. They have a variety of attractive thumbpieces by which they are usually dated. To about 1650 they had a simple wedge lying on the cover connecting with the hinge, and a ball or hammerhead sitting above the wedge as a thumb rest

Top Row: Pint and half-pint ale mugs as used in 19th century taverns and pubs.
Bottom Row: Measures used in the 19th century by a landlord for serving ales and spirits. The four measures in the centre were listed in an 1885 trade magazine as costing 4/6 for the quart, 4s for the pint, 3s for the half-pint and 2s for the gill. *Photograph: Christopher Sykes*

(this is sometimes missing, leading to dispute as to whether some early wedge types ever had the ball or hammerhead). From the mid-17th century thumbpieces were shaped like hammerheads or sprouting buds (known as the 'bud' thumbpiece). The next type was the 'double volute' so-named because of its resemblance to Ionic columns. This was common until the 19th century and was attached to the lid by a fleur-de-lys. On Scottish baluster measures thumbpieces were of a 'ball' type, or were shaped like an unformed shell without its radiating ridges (called the 'embryo-shell').

Both the tappit-hen and baluster measures were made in Imperial and Scots standard capacities. The former is also found with a crest or knob in the centre of the cover, without a knob and also lidless. The latter is known as the Aberdeen type and it has a hinge-lug unslotted for a hinge. Tappit-hens are seldom found with makers' marks.

Another attractive type of Scottish pewter vessel is a flagon, popular from the mid-18th century to the early 19th century, which is a cylinder type with slightly domed lid, a fillet moulding around the centre of the body and a widening out of the body into a skirt at the bottom. The lid fits neatly into the lip of the body by means of a flange on the underside, known as an 'anti-wobble' or a Scottish laver, and thus helps to prevent wear on the hinge when it moves loosely from side to side. The 'anti-wobble', which also appears on the Scottish baluster measure, may have originated in England as it is found on some early vessels.

There is a unique type of 18th-century flagon known as a York flagon which has an acorn-shaped body, a spout, a serrated lip to the cover and a handle of graceful sweeping proportions. Another attractive local type of vessel is the Guernsey measure, which has a flat heart-shaped cover and a pot-bellied body encircled with bands, and a long slender neck. It is similar to the Jersey measure which does not have the bands nor the distinct swelled-out base.

If I am dwelling too much on flagons and measures in a book on mugs and tankards, it is because all three types of vessel have to some extent been used interchangeably, and the amount of old pewter left is so little that those who admire the metal are frequently tempted to buy into other branches of the same family, many of which can be and are now used as mugs and tankards.

A flagon seen in English salerooms that is rather like the shape of the tappit-hen but with a 'Jan Steen' spout is the Bernese flagon. It has a domed lid, an erect or plume thumbpiece and a hooked handle.

In Ireland during the 19th century there were baluster measures without handles, a type called the 'noggin', made from the gallon down to the half-noggin, and the well-known haystack measures

Three 19th century pewter mugs sitting on a type of pewter drainer used in pubs. *Photograph: R. Mundey*

Left: Typical examples of English pewter ale mugs of the late 19th century with standard handles attached flat to the body at the lower end. These are still easy to obtain. *Photograph: Christopher Sykes Antiques*

Right: Rare example of a 19th century English pewter pint mug which has had the unusual feature of a copper band added to the top edge so that the landlord of a tavern could measure accurately without spilling any ale over the rim. *Photograph: Christopher Sykes Antiques*

named for their resemblance to the conical-top haystack. These latter are similar to a West Country variety of measure.

As the collecting of mugs and tankards is an increasingly international field, it is well to consider some further national variations. In early days, pewter styles were much the same in all European countries. But where the mark of the Tudor Rose and Crown is found, evidence shows that when makers' initials are in the crown or on the heart of the rose, they are Belgian, Dutch, French, German or Swiss. The same applies if the Rose and Crown mark is very small.

Another indication of pewter made in these countries, as opposed to Britain or America, is the appearance of three or more letters either in the maker's touch itself, in the Rose and Crown mark, or in a sort of imitation silver hallmark.

The Double Acorn thumbpiece is a Continental motif, as is a heart-shaped lid, except that these also appear on Channel Island vessels. A type of French flagon with a concave middle is sometimes confused with the Scottish tappit-hen, but will be found to have Continental characteristics.

A short, curtailed handle to an early flagon is German, compared with the fuller, wider sweep of the English handle terminating far down the body of the vessel. The Erect Thumbpiece which appears on German flagons will be seen to have a break in the curves both back and front that is not so apparent in English ones. The latter are also often pierced through with a heart-shaped pattern and the unmistakable sign – sweeping handles reaching far down the body compared with the short German handle – will be there

As with all categories of American antiques, America copied

Victorian half-pint pewter mug. Next to it is a turned wooden tankard-jack used in pubs to punch out the dents in a pewter mug. They were made in pint and half-pint sizes. *Photograph: Art and Antiques Weekly*

English styles in pewter and silver to begin with (often 75 to 100 years later) but, as time went on, developed characteristics unique to the Colonies. American pewterers were allowed greater latitude than their English forefathers in choosing the composition of their alloy, but laboured under the difficulties of large import duties on pewter from Cornwall – imposed under pressure from English pewterers who wished to keep the American market to themselves. As a result, American pewter was remade into new styles from older articles, and the stock of antiques accordingly diminished. Nevertheless, a surprising number of 18th-century tankards have survived, indicating how greatly prized they were at the time.

In 1693, the cost of a pewter quart tankard was 3s., of a half-gallon tankard 3s. 10d., and of a half-gallon wine measure 5s. 6d. This we know from a record in the Massachusetts archives of a shipment of pewter from England.

Although there was no guild in America to require the use of touchmarks, many makers chose to mark their wares in one way or another, as a matter of pride and a means of advertisement. Before the revolution the English-trained pewterers used such characteristic London symbols as the lion, rose, doves, columns,

Victorian trophy tankards made in a George II silver style. *Photograph: R. Mundey*

banners and cartouches; but when the War of Independence inspired patriotic zeal, the eagle found in the United States seal was much used. Sometimes a touchmark is ringed with stars.

A new vitality is emerging in the pewter industry today, encouraged by an active trade body – the Association of British Pewter Craftsmen – whose main aims are to encourage higher standards. A new trademark signifying quality in metal content and craftsmanship has been introduced for use by the 20-odd members of the Association. This is a triangle within a circle and the initials BPC in the centre. Great emphasis is being placed on improving standards by establishing a high quality of materials, design and craftsmanship.

Sales of pewter have increased enormously. New designs and finishes are encouraging younger people to buy pewterware for the table and for decoration. The warmth and softness of pewter in contrast to the harshness of stainless steel, the fragility of china and glass and the problems of cleaning silver, have all led to a new appreciation of this most traditional of English products.

Pewter has, for many years, suffered unfairly from criticism of its lead content and its dull or dirty appearance. In fact nowadays no lead is added to pewter, which consists of over 90 percent tin with a small amount of copper and antimony for hardening.

A very high sheen polish is now being given to most pewter goods, although there is still a strong demand for the older dark look of reproduction pewter, and some demand for a satin finish.

Pewter is produced in two ways: cast from molten metal in moulds, or spun and beaten from pewter sheet. Cast products are more expensive, as might be expected, being produced in tough moulds, many of them in traditional designs preserved for many hundreds of years. Spun pewter goods are produced from sheets of pewter, cut, formed and shaped into the wide variety of products now offered.

The pewter industry is established in Sheffield and Birmingham, where the majority of the members of the Association are located. In Sheffield, the industry is led by P.M.C. (Sheffield) Ltd., a substantial company which some years ago saw the potential of the pewter market and expanded to meet the vast demands of American

Three modern spun pewter tankards by Wardle and Matthews Ltd., Sheffield.
Left to right:
"Worcester" one-pint mug
"Old London" mug
"Charles I tankard"

A one-pint modern spun pewter mug designed for Haseler and Restall Ltd. (Birmingham) by Cade Designs.

buyers. P.M.C. probably have the biggest sales in the industry, producing a wide range of spun pewter, both for overseas orders and the growing English market.

But, despite the dominance of Sheffield and Birmingham as centres for manufacture, two of the leading firms in the pewter industry are based in the South East, Englefields in London and Aquinas Locke in Bedfordshire and London.

Englefields can trace a history of pewter manufacture back to 1700, and they produce a vast range of very high quality cast tankards, goblets, vases and gift items. Their 'Crown & Rose' pewter is in tremendous demand abroad.

Because pewter has been greatly appreciated for many years, it has also been greatly faked. The inexperienced can but buy from experienced collectors or dealers (securing a written description, so the dealer must commit himself under the Trades Description Act) for nearly *everything* worth *anything* gets faked. The popularity of mugs and tankards makes them principal targets. Experienced collectors rely on their own abilities to gauge with the eye whether an item looks 'right' (e.g., the style relates to the alleged period) and the patina is a result of genuine wear and age.

Chapter Four
POTTERY

The pleasing shape of the mug has made it one of the most popular mediums for commemorating events and people. Mugs and tankards throughout the 19th and 20th centuries have celebrated Coronations and other royal events, military and naval victories, political occasions, the births of relatives, sporting contests, famous personalities, centenaries, industrial landmarks such as the building of the railways, etc. Today, more than ever, commemoratives are big business. Manufacturers take advantage of the present-day fascination with history, and a widespread longing for the past and desire to slow down the fast course of recent history by stopping to mark national, international and local events. There is nothing like a date, face or picture to immortalize the mug or tankard as much as the occasion commemorated! Such an object has a specific function far removed from that of simply holding liquid.

The most common material for commemorative mugs is, of course, pottery. The development of creamware by Josiah Wedgwood in the early 1760s for the first time provided a pottery that could easily be mass-produced; and the technique of transfer-printing invented by John Sadler in 1756 made large-scale decoration possible. The design was engraved on a copper plate. Next, it was inked and a thin piece of paper laid on the plate to pick up the impression. This was then transferred on to the pot and the paper taken off, leaving the picture.

These new industrialized techniques were inspired by the increase in communication from town to town, mainly through the development of canals, roads and, eventually, the railways. Increased transportation meant not only the means to spread the news to be commemorated and the materials to make the mugs, but cheaper ways of doing both, so that the less than wealthy

Pottery mug commemorating social reformer George Kinloch. The inscription is "On the 22nd December 1819, forced to flee his country and proclaimed an outlaw for having advocated the cause of the people and the necessity of Reform. On 22nd December 1832 proclaimed the chosen representative of the town of Dundee in the Reform House of Commons. *Photograph: J. and J. May*

could afford to buy the objects to grace their mantelpieces.

John and Jennifer May, specialists in pottery commemoratives, have identified the ealiest pottery mug made actually to commemorate an event, rather than merely to show an image of a monarch, as a mug marking the coronation of Charles II in 1660. The artist apparently intended originally to show Cromwell, for the body is his, while the face has been hastily changed to that of Charles.[1]

This mug is, however, exceptional, for there was little commemorative pottery appearing until the conditions for a popular industry had been developed towards the end of the 18th century. One of the early subjects shown on mugs was the building of the famous Iron Bridge over the River Wear, opened in 1796, and this industrial feat is still being commemorated today on pottery. However, the first items illustrating it were probably made much later, in the 1820s.

Early creamware items often celebrated the sea or waterways in one way or another: Britain has always been much involved in terms of war and commerce with the sea, her sons have earned their livelihood on the water and undoubtedly many of the early commemorative mugs and tankards were sold at seaports and designed to appeal to sailors. One of the earliest commemorative subjects was thus Admiral Rodney who defeated the Spanish Fleet

[1] *Commemorative Pottery*, John and Jennifer May, Heinemann, p. 1.

off Cape St Vincent in 1780 during the American War of Independence. He was celebrated on mugs and other creamwares for this and the Battle of the Saintes a few months later.

Following the War of Independence was the war with France, from 1793 until the Battle of Waterloo in 1815. Nelson and Wellington, their lives and deaths, were frequently depicted on mugs and tankards, some of contemporary make and others made long after the events.

Strictly speaking, a commemorative in its purest form is made at or near the time of the event that inspired it. However, as we have become well aware in these modern times, retrospective commemoratives are extremely popular as well. Winston Churchill, the granting of the County of Bristol's Charter, the founding of Bath, Charles Dickens and the voyage of the *Mayflower* are

Right: Commemorative pottery mug, late 18th century, depicting the pickpocket Barrington who was sent to Botany Bay and later became a High Sheriff in Australia. *Photograph: J. and J. May*

Left: Boxing was often commemorated in the late 18th and early 19th centuries. This pottery mug shows a transfer print of Humphreys and Mendoza fighting at Odiham, Hampshire in 1788. *Photograph: J. and J. May*

Left: Many century advances were honoured on 19th century pottery mugs such as the construction of bridges, in this case London Bridge. *Photograph: J. and J. May*

Right: Splendid transfer-print of The Great Eastern Steam-ship, circa 1840. *Photograph: J. and J. May*

just some of the excuses that have been found recently for issuing new commemorative mugs and tankards.

Modern commemoratives really got into gear with the Coronation of Edward VII in 1902, and they have been mass-produced for every coronation since, including those of George V in 1911, George VI in 1937, Queen Elizabeth in 1953 and even Edward VIII in 1936. Although the last-named abdicated before his coronation could take place, many commemoratives to mark the coming event were already on the market; they are, therefore, not rarities. Royal anniversaries, marriages and other events have been well-

64

19th century pottery mug from Australia inscribed "A Present From Cole's Book Arcade Melbourne." *Photograph: J. and J. May*

remembered and none more so than the Investiture of the Prince of Wales on July 1st 1969 and the wedding of Princess Anne and Captain Mark Phillips on November 14th 1973. The Prince of Wales is pretty certain to become king and to retain his popularity, though one wonders if the Princess and her husband will always enjoy the intense public interest aroused on that occasion! The wedding mug illustrated is in many ways an ideal commemorative, for it is extremely attractive, in modern shades of blue and red; and it contains many symbols representing the couple – horses and riders, trees symbolising the countryside they love so well, the Abbey where they were married, hearts, the rising sun for youth and even the Royal Yacht *Britannia* away in the distance. This was not specified as a limited edition, but, as is often the case with commemoratives, it became, due to a variety of circumstances, a very small issue – about 130. Each mug cost £6.48, including VAT, new. The sponsors of the mug, J. and J. May, added to the last batch of 30 the words 'Preserved From Assassina-

Friendly Society mugs such as this one (two views) often have charming primitive designs but commemorative collectors are not very keen about them and they are therefore inexpensive. This dates from about 1830. *Photograph: J. and J. May*

Left: Collectors of cartoons would appreciate this satire on Napoleon's new role as Emperor. *Photograph: J. and J. May*

Right: Rare Newcastle Pottery mug commemorating death of Nelson. Queen Victoria, Wellington and Nelson are probably the three most sought-after subjects in antique commemoratives. *Photograph: J. and J. May*

tion 20 March 1974'. These làst, at £8.64 including VAT, well illustrate one of the main principles governing good commemoratives: record a significant event *as it happens*.

A great many mugs have celebrated English military achievements. A mug showing Lord Earl Howe, Commander of the British Fleet, may commemorate the breaking of the French line on The Glorious First of June in 1794, or his appointment as Commander-in-Chief. There are mugs showing Sir John Jervis, hero of the Battle of St Vincent, when Nelson first came into the limelight, then as Earl St Vincent. Nelson's first victory was the Battle of the Nile, but this was not well-commemorated, though there is one mug showing the battle taking place and bearing the inscription

'The Young Alexander of France
May boast of his power in vain
When Nelson appears 'tis confessed
That Britons are Lords of the main.'

The Peace of Amiens is celebrated on mugs made by the Bristol pottery, showing the female figures of peace and plenty, the flags of England and France and the inscription 'Peace signed at Amiens between England, France, Spain and Holland March 27 1802'.

Nelson and Queen Victoria are the two favourite subjects of commemorative collectors, and probably the mug and tankard collector will aim to represent them both in his collection. There is a rare frog mug commemorating Nelson's death, for instance, decorated with pink lustre. For the uninitiated, frog mugs are simply that – pottery mugs with ceramic frogs stuck and fired on to the inside, usually on the lower side, sometimes partly splayed on the bottom.

There were many other types of mugs made at the time of Nelson's death and even long afterwards. One shows a portrait of Nelson within a circular cartouche and is inscribed ('England expects every man will do his duty').

With the Peninsula Wars and the rise to fame of Wellington, the great day for naval victories was largely over and attention was turned to the land. Pottery commemoratives followed his victories and various honours preceding his elevation to Duke.

Pottery mugs were not treated with the same respect as porcelain or ornamental wares and were, therefore, broken in vast numbers. Although commemoratives were not used to the same extent as ordinary drinking vessels, they nevertheless took a high toll of breakages.

Royal commemoratives remain the perennial favourites, the coronation mug for Queen Victoria being the archetype of all pottery commemoratives. Most collectors aim to have one, but as these are fairly hard to find nowadays (and their very rarity is, of course, why they are so keenly sought), relatively few are successful. There are three transfers generally used for both Proclamation and Coronation mugs. The two most common both show a bust of the Queen wearing a low-cut dress, necklace and pendant, and they are distinguished mainly by the way the necklace and pendant lie. In one, from the Swansea factory, the necklace comes straight around the neck with a plain round pendant; and in the other, the necklace bends around the neck and terminates in a scalloped pendant. The rarest transfer shows a three-quarter length figure of the Queen wearing the same low-cut dress, but with a triple row of pearls around her neck and a high plaited bun

Anything with railway themes is enormously popular, such as these three pottery mugs made in the height of the 19th century railway boom. *Photograph: J. and J. May*

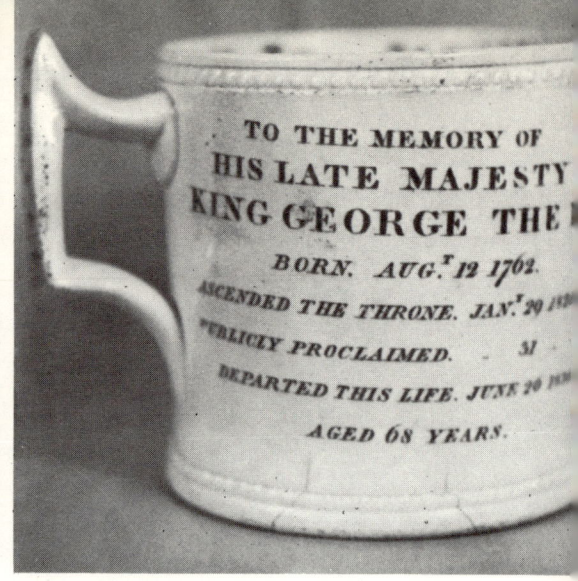

Right: Pottery mug of about 1840 showing Queen Victoria and Prince Albert. May have been made for a specific event but it does not say. *Photograph: J. and J. May*

Left: George IV has gone down in history as one of the least mourned of all sovereigns. His passing was also little commemorated, but this is one lasting memory to the scandulous king. *Photograph: J. and J. May*

without ringlets. Usually her mother, the Duchess of Kent, also appears on the mug.

There are other prints of the Queen on mugs about the time of the Coronation, which may be regarded as Ascension or Coronation mugs, though they do not specify it. One is a blue transfer simply inscribed 'Victoria Regina', bearing a waist-length portrait of the Queen wearing a veil, earrings, necklace and shawl with Windsor Castle in the background.

From then on, there were a great many mugs depicting the Queen, her husband or children. Some were made purely for local distribution and are, therefore, rare.

Animal mugs, children's mugs and miniatures are always favourites with those whose tastes run to novelties. Children and animals were well catered for in Victorian times, from which most examples come. A pair of small creamware loving cups of 1802 and 1804 which I have seen each contains a ceramic frog and bears the name of Peter Bates. I feel certain that Peter was a lad of about five and seven years old in 1802 and 1804 respectively, and pampered enough to be given these juvenile jokes – the second, undoubtedly, on his request.

There are a fair number of small mugs surviving from the 19th century to attest to contemporary pious attitudes to children. They bear transfer prints of lessons on the Alphabet, biblical verses and moral sayings, pictures of sports and animals, inscriptions such as 'A Present for My Niece', and illustrations of games such as Hunt the Slipper. These and a variety of other subjects were depicted on 'pint-sized' mugs which were considerably smaller than pints. Richer families lavished silver mugs on their children.

Mentioned previously was the frog mug. This was a huge joke, popular with sailors, children and others, and one that is still popular today. The earliest known examples date from about 1775–1780 and they have continued to be made up to the present, both legitimately and as fakes. Some say they were meant to frighten unsuspecting guests while drinking their beer, and others have speculated that the frog represents the demon drink. Antique ones usually cost more than frogless equivalents. They were made in creamware by such potteries as Sunderland and Leeds and in cruder country earthenwares.

Extremely popular with adults were the Toby jugs which, symbolised the love of ale. As they were often made with a cup in the tricorne hat from which to drink one's ale, they can also qualify as a type of mug (modern reproductions are sometimes made as

Left: Fairly rare to find but keenly sought by commemorative collectors is a Queen Victoria coronation mug such as this one, not dated but probably made for the coronation in 1838. *Photograph: J. and J. May*

Right: A locally issued pottery mug commemorating Queen Victoria's Golden Jubilee. *Photograph: J. and J. May*

Above left: Pottery mug commemorating marriage of Duke of York and Princess May in 1893. A number of popular items were made for this event. Later of course the couple became King George V and Queen Mary. *Photograph: J. and J. May*

Above right: Pottery mug commemorating marriage of Prince Albert Edward (later Edward VII) and Princess Alexandra on March 10, 1863. *Photograph: J. and J. May*

Below: Two views of a two-handled pottery mug or loving cup circa 1840 with a hunting theme popular with collectors who like the sport. *Photograph: J. and J. May*

drinking mugs). Primarily, however, the portrait character of the Toby jug normally makes it a favourite candidate for the mantelpiece.

The idea of portraying people in pottery goes back to pre-historic times, but the inspiration behind the 18th-century Toby jug, which is popular in antique, reproduction, and modern versions to this day, was not Shakespeare's Sir Toby Belch nor Lawrence Sterne's Uncle Toby (from *Tristram Shandy*), but rather the great glutton Toby Filpot, the nickname for Henry Elwes, a star drunkard of the 18th century who is said to have consumed 2,000 gallons of strong ale in his life-time.

So popular was the finely modelled Toby that it has been immortalized in literature, passed down to succeeding generations as an important family heirloom, and continually imitated. Some of the most recent versions include representations of Winston Churchill and Graham Hill.

The original Toby was the very model of a Georgian gentleman, albeit an immoderately greedy one. He is well-dressed in a man's outsize long coat and waistcoat, knee-breeches and stockings, shoes with buckles or strings, and a cravat. But the two important accessories are the tricorne hat and a jug or mug of ale on his knee. In the original mezzotint he is shown with a jug of ale foaming on top, and with the clay pipe often found on the pottery models.

A poem about Toby which appeared in 1761 runs:
'His body, when long in the Ground had lain
And time into Clay had resolv'd it again
A potter found out in its Covert so snug
And with part of fat Toby form'd this brown jug'.

This verse and the engraving inspired Ralph Wood of Burslem to manufacture the jugs from about 1765 onwards.

It is not certain who actually made the first Toby jug, but Ralph Wood examples are most sought-after by collectors. However, if this firm was the first, others very quickly followed suit, until a wide range was available, from the traditional Toby to the Collier and the Thin Man, the Sailor and the Parson, and jugs featuring contemporary notables such as Martha Gunn, the well-known Brighton bathing attendant who is said to have taught the then Prince of Wales to swim. She is sometimes depicted with his three-feather emblem, but she is also unfairly shown with a gin bottle. There is a Bluff King Hal Toby, said to represent the Prince Regent,

The outside and inside views of a 19th century pottery frog mug meant originally as an amusing novelty or to frighten the unsuspecting drinker as he drained his cup. This is a pink lustre "ODD FELLOWS AND FORESTERS" mug. The frog is black and yellow. Frog mugs are usually more expensive than their frogless equivalents. *Photograph: Sotheby's*

71

A child's pottery mug with silver lustre borders and transfer-printed decoration reading "A Reward for Industry" and including view of Enoch Wood's factory at Burslem, circa 1840, 3 inches high. *Photograph: Geoffrey Godden, chinaman*

Children's 19th century pottery mugs with animal and sporting subjects, 2½ inches high. *Photograph: J. and J. May*

later King George IV, who dressed as Henry VIII at a Brighton masquerade.

Toby jugs of the 18th century rarely took national heroes for subjects, as they did in Victorian times and do today; but one was made to represent Lord Howe. It was a Ralph Wood design, in which the admiral is seated on a barrel with a pipe at his side and a dog at his feet.

Other well-known names in this field were Wedgwood, Whieldon, Enoch Wood, Astbury and Felix Pratt. The first four firms, as well as Ralph Wood I (1715–1772) and Ralph Wood II (1745–1795), made Toby jugs in the 18th century which are renowned for their fine modelling and good colour. However, a famous 19th-century name in Toby jugs was Felix Pratt's firm, and today Royal

Children's pottery mug, circa 1880, in honour of the founder of the Sunday school movement. *Photograph: J. and J. May*

Doulton make a fine series.

Georgian Tobys cost only a few pence to shillings, but today's Georgian survivals cost three figures for fine examples. Beware of fakes, for the current value of original Tobys has encouraged the making of spurious figures.

Some early miniatures exist which may have been made purely for decoration, or as concessions to the temperance movement.

Similar to Toby jugs were the Staffordshire face mugs of the 18th century and later, which also did not feature many actual people until more recently. These were also made in porcelain.

Probably the most amusing face mugs are those made by the Martin Brothers – Robert Wallace, Edwin, Walter and Charles Martin – about 1900. These and their stoneware face jugs and absurd birds are among the most sought-after of all pottery at the moment, being among the best of the class of 'Studio Potters' of the late 19th century associated with the 'back to craftsmanship' movement inspired and led by William Morris. Their mugs are extremely finely modelled and it is a euphemism to say that they are highly individual.

Also in the tradition of individually made stonewares were those by Hannah Barlow and other artists working for Doulton. The name of Doulton goes back to about 1820, when it was associated with the making of utilitarian objects, such as ginger beer bottles. In the 1860s, however, the firm began an honorable tradition of artist-made pottery. Hannah Barlow's works are all unique

Two sizes of pottery mugs with a delightful transfer commemorating the visit of an American lion tamer Mr. Van Amburgh in the late 1830s. *Photograph: J. and J. May*

and are all signed with her initials, H.B.B., in monogram form. Designs were made by incised lines coloured with pigments. She was famous for her spirited animal studies, combined with a beautiful simplicity in their placing on the vessels.

Throughout the history of pottery from about 1500 BC in China, stonewares have ranked among the most practical. They are made from tough clays which vitrify at high temperatures without collapsing, thereby becoming impermeable to liquids. European stonewares date from about 1300 in Germany, where, in the latter half of the 15th century, saltglazing was discovered.

Stoneware was perfected in England at the Fulham Pottery in the early 1670s. Made in this hard, vitrified, durable pottery were attractive bulbous-shaped mugs with cylindrical necks similar to Rhenish stoneware mugs and to those found in silver about the same time. Cylindrical mugs were commonly made at Fulham, and both general shapes were made at a number of other potteries. They were decorated with applied, incised and relief designs. There were even tankards made with stoneware covers.

Staffordshire stoneware mugs were evidently used in taverns in the 18th century, for there are examples bearing official capacity seals impressed into the body and the marks of the reigning monarchs, such as Queen Anne and a Georgian 'G.R.'.

Victorian pottery mug with a doggy theme. *Photograph: J. and J. May*

Stonewares hold great beauty for those who admire their simple ruggedness and natural clay colours. However, they have also been decorated with colours in various ways and by no means all stoneware is rough or crude. Besides his creamware mentioned earlier, Josiah Wedgwood's black basalt and jasperware brought into existence two other media not only for use as commemoratives, but as fine tablewares and decorative items. Jasper and black basalt were refined stonewares fit for kings.

These were popular materials for mugs, as well as other articles, and were developed by Josiah Wedgwood in the second half of the 18th century. They have continued in production to this day. Wedgwood was by no means alone in producing fine vessels in these materials and there are extremely fine examples that bear no factory mark at all. (The Wedgwood firm, of course, usually marked theirs, except for minor pieces, in a set). Basalt was a hard,

Two views of children's pottery mug circa 1790 showing that "Hunt the Slipper" has amused Georgians, Victorians and 20th century children alike, 2½ inches high. *Photograph: J. and J. May*

Two Victorian pottery children's mugs, circa 1820-1860, one an alphabet mug declaring "D IS A DOG THE FRIEND OF THE HOUSE" and the other also instructive with "B was a Butcher, and Kept a Great Dog." Photograph: J. and J. May

fine-grained black unglazed stoneware suitable for polishing on lathes and engine-turning. Basalt wares were usually decorated with moulded reliefs in a classical vein.

Wedgwood's greatest contribution to pottery may arguably have been his creamware, as it provided a refined earthenware capable of taking all manner of decorations and transfers; and, most important, it could be afforded by the mass of people. But his Jasperware was his most creative achievement, the result of many arduous experiments. Wedgwood himself described Jasper as

> A white porcelain biscuit of exquisite beauty and delicacy, possessing the general properties of the basaltes, together with that of receiving colours through its whole surface, in a manner which no other body, ancient or modern, has been known to do. This renders it peculiarly fit for cameos, portraits and all subjects in bas-relief; as the ground may be made of any colour throughout, without paint or enamel, and the raised figures of a pure white.[2]

His jaspers come in blue, white, lilac, various greens including turquoise, crimson, buff and other colours.

[2] *Wedgwood Jasper* by Robin Reilly, Charles Letts & Co., p. 11.

Victorian child's pottery mug circa 1820-60 appealing to collectors of animal mugs. This is unusual for having a "named" dog on it, Pompey. *Photograph: J. and J. May*

While many jaspers are coloured throughout ('solid jasper'), others were only tinted on the surface and known as 'jasper-dip'. The mugs made in this way have a formal, classical appeal and seem rather far from the atmosphere of a hardy ale-drinking crowd.

Rather more earthy-looking were the mugs made in a similar body to jasper and decorated similarly with reliefs, but with the main difference that they were left their natural buff colour. John Turner (1738–1787), a Staffordshire potter, made many mugs of this type, often decorated additionally with a silver rim by which one can, by means of the hallmark, date the item, and he is credited with developing this particular slightly-glossy porcelainous stoneware. Other potters produced similar mugs. Some used a matt body and others a slightly glazed one.

It is unlikely that one will be able to add many pre-18th-century

Children's Victorian alphabet mugs, circa 1820-60. P is for Puppy, H is for Hound. *Photograph: J. and J. May*

This is an engraving of the glutton on whom the famous 18th century Toby jug is modelled, Toby Fillpot, the nickname of Henry Elwes a Yorkshire drunkard who is said to have consumed 2,000 gallons of strong ale before he died in 1761. *Photograph: Art and Antiques Weekly*

pottery mugs and tankards to a collection. As an eminently utilitarian and expendable substance, pottery was discarded when broken or chipped. However, its inter-relatedness with the more durable silver and pewter makes it interesting to study, even if not possible to own.

While mugs and tankard shapes in all materials may have derived from the same primitive pottery base, in later years when the various crafts existed side-by-side they influenced each other, with the most fashionable material tending to lead the way. However, sometimes fervent attempts at pinpointing influences can trap one into a ridiculous chicken-and-egg situation. Hence, early English delft mugs were thought to have been influenced by the globular shapes of Rhenish stoneware, which had inspired the silversmiths in England who, in the 17th and 18th centuries, in turn set the fashionable shapes for delft.

Left: A rare Toby jug by Ralph Wood called "The Collier," 10 inches high.
Centre: A rare and unusual "Thin Man" Toby jug, 9¾ inches high.
Right: Typical Toby jug by Ralph Wood, 9¾ inches high. *Photograph: Sotheby's*

A typically fine quality marked Turner face mug, circa 1790, 4¼ inches high. *Photograph: Geoffrey Godden, chinaman*

But in fact long before English delftware began to be made, in the mid-16th century, English potters were at work producing slipwares (a technique of adding a decorative coating to pottery by means of 'slips' of diluted and coloured clays) and other rough earthenware for use at table by the people of the Middle Ages – of course, pottery has been made since time immemorial. The basic rounded, bulbous and cylindrical shapes, spun naturally from a slab of clay on the potter's wheel or fashioned by primitive man by depressing the centre of a ball of clay, were borrowed by makers of vessels of wood, leather, glass, pewter and silver and, naturally, by workers with pottery's first cousin, porcelain – not to mention by succeeding generations of potters.

There is little, in my opinion, to equal the charm of English delft. Yet there is also little that equals it for impracticality, compared with the later creamwares and porcelains. The clay body was prone to crumbling and the tin-glaze covering easily cracked and chipped, so that the body absorbed the liquids and became unhygienic. Nevertheless, as collector's items, English delft mugs have a special delicacy of design and colouring, and there are still a few 18th-century mugs available on the market.

Although England already had a long history of pottery-making, the development of tin-glazed earthenware was welcomed because it was the nearest approximation at the time to the much-vaunted Chinese porcelain. The covering white glazes containing tin ashes were virtually the same in Dutch Delft and French and German faience and not much different from their origins in Italian maiolica. Decorations often imitated oriental floral plants, birds and insect motifs.

The first English delft mugs seem to have been made, from about 1550, in the globular shape with cylindrical necks of the Rhenish stoneware mugs then being imported and applied with English silver and pewter mounts. These delft mugs and jugs were also given silver or silver-gilt mounts.

A barrel-shaped delft mug was made from about 1628 onwards, which F. H. Garner and Michael Archer writing in *English Delftware*[3] liked to call one of the first truly English wares of their kind. This may indeed have been the inspiration for the 18th-century and early 19th-century barrel mugs found in silver and pewter . . . but again I digress into circular arguments.

Cylindrical mugs existed at the same time, and a few years later the globular form with a cylindrical neck similar to the Rhenish stoneware prototypes appears again.

In the 18th century, the earliest form was straight-sided with

[2] *English Delftware* by F. H. Garner and Michael Archer Faber & Faber, p. 6.

Humorous face mug made by the Martin Brothers studio potters from 1873 to about 1915. *Photograph: Sotheby's*

Doulton buff-coloured salt-glazed stoneware mugs with incised animal decorations by the famous decorator of the firm Hannah Barlow circa 1872. *Photograph: Richard Dennis*

a few rings around the bottom similar to stoneware mugs made at Lambeth and Fulham. Another type was cylindrical, with a flared base, found in pewter and silver. From the middle of the century bell-shaped mugs appeared which are also seen in silver, pewter, glass and porcelain; and the latest form before the making of English delft ceased was a mug with a slightly flared base, which sometimes had a glass bottom.

Contemporary with English delft were the 17th and 18th century slipwares made in the Staffordshire potteries and elsewhere. These are among the most charming examples of 'country' pottery ever made: look for instance for the cylindrical mugs with sgraffiato decoration of animals and leaves incised in dark brown slip and covered with warm brown glaze.

So many different types of pottery in the 18th century provided variegated mugs and tankards. Agate, veined or marbled wares were made which, due to the technique of wedging several different colours of clay together, produced a decorative effect that required no more embellishment.

Thomas Whieldon, famous Staffordshire potter, is associated with various pottery techniques, but with none more than a type of ware coloured with warm semi-translucent glazes, often mottled in effect. This type of glazed pottery was used by others, including the Ralph Wood pottery from which emanated Toby jugs coloured with these glazes.

Transfer-printed commemorative and other wares have already been discussed, but without mention of the important colour-printed Pratt wares. Felix Pratt may or may not have been the first to put polychrome transfers on pottery, but he was the main specialist and certainly the most famous. The results of his colour-printing are generally considered far superior to those of his rivals.

The technique required engraving a copper plate for each colour, including the black outline, and taking a print from each and superimposing one upon the other, in perfect register. These very attractive wares, dating from about the 1840s, have been rather overlooked because of the publicity and high prices accorded Pratt's now-famous pot lids on meat and fish paste and cosmetic jars.

An asset to a collection of mugs and tankards would be one of the Mocha ware mugs made throughout the 19th century and often used in taverns. They are characterized by markings of pigments, often brown, but also blue, green and black, and by

Staffordshire engine-turned basalt mug with inlaid borders, circa 1780–90, 5½ inches high.
Photograph: Geoffrey Godden, chinaman

Majolica pot or mug made in the Netherlands circa 1550 and excavated from Nonsuch Palace near Ewell in Surrey in 1969-70.

feathery tree- and fern-like plants created by a simple chemical reaction. An acid colourant such as tobacco or hops was applied to an alkaline ground colour, and rapidly formed a decorative growth. Early ones from the late 18th century were made in creamware, and from about 1820 in pearlware and, later, stoneware. Factories involved in their production were, among others, Leeds Pottery (where they were termed 'Moscha'), Spode and C. T. Maling of Newcastle.

The Leeds factory was responsible for many of the attractive and high-quality products of its time. The firm produced superb creamware (some say the finest) covered with smooth, brilliant, creamy glazes of greenish-yellow tone. Fine basalts were made, silver and pink lustres, red stoneware, tortoiseshell ware and many transfer-printed items, of which mugs were most popular. Much was exported in competition with Wedgwood in the late 18th century.

Most of the best ceramic wares used in early America came from abroad, where they were often made with American themes and taste in mind. The Americans themselves made rather cruder wares such as redware until the 19th century, when fine earthenwares and porcelain were made to match the imported European articles.

All the ingredients existed in America for the making of fine potteries and porcelains; yet little was made in the 17th and 18th centuries, for although the colonists liked to think of themselves as patriotic, they were snobbish enough to prefer the imported European product.

On the home front, the popular useful wares were coarse redware folk pottery produced by many small potteries. These were washed or splashed in glazes of browns, yellows, oranges, pinks, brownish-black and copper-greens. These often bore incised or 'scratched' decorations ('sgraffiato'), especially in Pennsylvania, where traditional European peasant designs were transplanted so charmingly to the New World. Saltglazed stonewares were also made in abundance, but were of finer and denser clays and were stronger than in Europe, due to being fired at higher temperatures. Their colours ranged from grey to buff to dark brown. The favourite decoration was hand-painting in cobalt blue or, occasionally, brown. Toby jugs of stoneware were also made.

Although one David Henderson of Jersey City was commended for his stoneware Toby jugs in buff and brown in 1829–1830, American potters on the whole did not enjoy high status (as silversmiths and pewterers did). This was notably so in the 18th

English delft straight-sided mug in the London Museum, with blue handle and narrow blue bands around the rim and base, and with bird, rock and foliage decoration in the Ming tradition. It is inscribed "JAMES AND ELIZABETH GREENE ANNO 1630. THE GIFT IS SMALL GOODWILL IS ALL." *Photograph: London Museum*

A stoneware relief-decorated mug 5¾ inches high, circa 1795, marked "Turner." *Photograph: Geoffrey Godden, chinaman*

century when Wedgwood's creamware ('Queensware') could not be matched for popularity by anything the local denizens were inspired to make.

Mocha ware mugs were imported, but a similar 'Moco ware' was made after 1850 by Edwin Bennett of Baltimore.

Any pottery from the Art and Studio Potteries of the turn of this century is keenly sought, but mugs much less than vases and other large items. So if one confines one's search purely to mugs by well-known makers such as Doulton and the Martin Brothers and by a few lesser-known art-potteries, such as Ault, Aller-Vale and Farnham one may continue to spend a fraction of what one would spend on the more decorative pieces. Equally one may concentrate on mugs in art nouveau, for the mug hardly lends

Staffordshire potter John Turner (1738-87) made beautiful stonewares of a buff-colour decorated with relief figures and silver or silver-plated rims. This is a fine example, circa 1800, 6¼ inches high, with a Sheffield rim and the mug is marked "Turner." Leading potters of the 1785-1825 era copied these relief-decorated wares. *Photograph: Geoffrey Godden, chinaman*

A marked Davenport stoneware mug of the 1815 period with hunting scene in relief, 4¼ inches high. *Photograph: Geoffrey Godden, chinaman*

A red-ground colour-printed Pratt-ware two-handled pottery mug, circa 1860-70, 5 inches high. *Photograph: Geoffrey Godden, chinaman*

Pottery presentation mug painted with typical pink lustre scenic design, 1820, 5½ inches high. *Photograph: Geoffrey Godden, chinaman*

Wemyss ware pottery cider mug circa 1900 decorated with cherries. Hand-painted items brightly decorated with flowers, fruit, insects, animals and birds were made at the Fife Pottery in Gallatown, nr. Kirkcaldy Scotland from the 1880s to 1930. Among the famous collectors of this ware were President Franklin Roosevelt and the present Queen Mother. Most bear the factory mark, either impressed or a hand-painted script, except in the case of sets in which only the main pieces might carry the mark. Collectors rarely touch unmarked items and prefer to see Wemyss impressed which is not easily faked. Collection of Geoffrey Harley. *Photograph: by Ian Wainwright*

Wedgwood one-pint pottery mug commemorating the 350th anniversary of the sailing of the Pilgrim Fathers on the Mayflower. With an all-over decoration in soft nutmeg brown, the design depicts the Pilgrim Fathers leaving Plymouth on one side of the mug, a description of the event on the reverse and the spine of an early copy of the Bible. It cost 49/6d in 1970.

itself to writhing, tendril shapes and remains one of the less sought-after collector's items.

As for art deco and modern pottery, a collector will have unlimited scope, for the vibrant, geometrical shapes and colours of art deco and the back-to-nature simple modern stonewares

Modern commemorative mug by Wedgwood in Queen's ware for 900th aniversary of Lincoln Cathedral, one of a series from Wedgwood recording events and people in English history. The colouring is yellow ochre and black, with a red line encircling the rim which bears the inscription "Bishop Remigius Began Building Lincoln Cathedral in 1072; It was Consecrated on Ascension Day 1092." Price new in 1972 was £3·95

Prince of Wales Investiture pottery mug by Wedgwood. The designer Carl Toms adapted an early 19th century print of Caernarvon Castle for the black and white design on this one-pint mug. When being sold around the time of the Investiture July July 1, 1969 the cost was 44/9p. It was not made in a limited edition.

are in striking contrast in style, but share the common denominator of being inexpensive.

Most 19th-century and 20th-century pottery mugs will be signed, so one will be able to distinguish the art deco works of Clarice Cliff, Pilkington, Poole Pottery, Thomas Forester and Sons, James Sadler and Sons, and countless others producing pottery in the 1920s and 1930s. Sunbursts, stylized flowers and fruits, geometric shapes and bold, bright colours and designs are among the characteristic features of art deco.

A type of bold hand-painted pottery that is not to be confused with art deco is that made at the Fife Pottery in Gallatown, near Kirkcaldy in Scotland, from the 1880s to 1930. Wemyss ware was loved by Franklin D. Roosevelt and is said to be collected by the Queen Mother. Actually, Roosevelt collected Wemyss pigs, which are unlikely creatures covered in gigantic sprays of roses. Favourite decorations on mugs are flowers and fruits, painted in bright colours on white. There is also a type known as 'gaudy' Wemyss, which is totally coloured, with a bright yellow occurring frequently. Wemyss was expensive when made and is still expensive, as it is difficult to find. Collectors always look for the impressed 'Wemyss' mark as a sign of authenticity, as the ware has been faked and reproduced with printed marks – though some items with printed marks are also genuine.

Two views of a pottery mug commemorating the wedding of Princess Anne and Captain Mark Phillips November 14, 1973. The design by Clifford Richards for J. and J. May commemorative specialists includes a bit of everything connected with the couple: horses, trees symbolising the country, the abbey where they were married, the rising sun representing youth and even a picture of the royal yacht *Britannia* in the distance. Colours are red, white and blue. Although not specified as a limited edition, only about 130 were made due to various unforeseen circumstances, and the last 30 or so also commemorated the attack on the couple in March 1974, reading "Preserved from Assassination 20 March 1974." With the latter the mugs cost £8·64 including VAT and the ordinary ones were £6·48. Photograph: J. and J. May

Chapter Five
PORCELAIN

Europeans were very pleased with themselves indeed when they learned the secret of making fine white porcelain like the Chinese. Although rarely quite the same – and a good thing too, because new bodies, styles and colours were created that were equally beautiful – the products of the European factories were made to extremely high standards and those who could afford it rushed to buy their excellent achievements. Pride in the successes of their factories in approximating a material and decoration that had long been regarded as precious and the epitomy of human endeavour, led Europeans to want many of the prized items of tableware to be made of the new porcelains – including mugs and tankards.

The European porcelain makers were at first more intent on imitation than originality. Not only did they try to copy Chinese and Japanese motifs and techniques such as those ubiquitous Chinese scenes and flowering shrubs in blue and white, but they copied the fashionable silver and pewter shapes of the day. The squat mugs and tankards, the cylindrical forms, the tapering straight-sided vessels and the bell shapes traditional to metal work, were all copied. However, two factors made western porcelain mugs and tankards unique. First, the Orientals did not drink their beverages from such vessels. And second, the vivid and delicate colourings that were achieved on porcelain, combined with the fineness of the china, could not be achieved on silver, pewter, wood, leather, glass or even pottery. Thus, the European porcelain mug or tankard is indeed its own creation. And what a novelty it must have been to enjoy one's favourite ale or beer in such finery!

Mugs and tankards were made by most 18th- and 19th-century porcelain manufacturers, and each pattern might come in

Meissen porcelain tankard with silver-gilt lid bearing Augsburg mark of J. E. Heuglin II, 1723. The porcelain shows a Chinoiserie river landscape painted by J. G. Herold. A medallion on the lid representing Africa is taken from the Four Continents theme that appears in porcelain. The thumbpiece is in the form of two grotesque-headed animals. *Photograph: Winifred Williams*

several different sizes. Sometimes mugs were made to match jugs, and as both mugs and jugs were popular presents both might be decorated with the initial of the owner. Handles as well as decorations would be the same, so that if one were to find a jug attributable to a particular factory one might assume the possible existence of mugs of similar form.

Although many tankards were made, few have survived with their lids intact. So a number of vessels which may well once have qualified for the title 'tankard' are today no more than mugs, despite the fondness dealers and auctioneers have for calling everything a tankard because it sounds more expensive.

The flat decoration on porcelain mugs and tankards was normally either painted or printed, over or under the glaze. Decoration over the glaze requires refiring so that it fuses with the surface. So-called underglaze decoration refers to metallic pigments, such as cobalt (blue), manganese (purple or brown), copper (green), antimony (yellow) and iron (red), capable of being fired at extremely high temperatures; these are applied to the body before the glaze was applied and then baked at about 1200–1400 degrees Centigrade.

The Meissen factory was the hero of the European scene, the first successful producer of hard-paste porcelain, from which other European factories took their cue, and eventually Chinese porcelain took its cue in turn when designing for the European market. However, as Meissen was for a time known only to the nobility and was, in fact, prohibited from commercial import into this country, it was the Chinese and Japanese porcelain imported directly by the British East India Company that was first influential in England.

An early Meissen tankard of white hard-paste porcelain in imitation of the Chinese "Blanc-de-Chine." It is decorated with applied flower and leaf sprigs and the lid of pewter is dated 1708. However, this may have been fitted later. The porcelain was made circa 1715 and the whole tankard including lid and thumb-piece measures 14cm. *Photograph: Winifred Williams.*

Early Meissen chinoiserie tankard in the manner of J. G. Herold with domed silver cover. *Photograph: Christie's*

Meissen developed hard-paste 'true' porcelain in the early years of the 18th century. One of their first products was the plain white porcelain, unembellished with other colours, except silver or silver-gilt mounts in tankards, in order to show off the achievement of the pure white porcelain bodies. In fact, white can come in many different colours and the early white wares of Meissen, Doccia, Mennecy, Vincennes, St Cloud and Chantilly can vary from grey to cream, to snow, to milk. These were in imitation of the Chinese 'blanc de Chine', a white porcelain made at Te Hua for export mainly to European countries during the 15th–18th centuries. The Meissen factory was established in 1710 near Dresden by Augustus the Strong, Elector of Saxony, following experiments carried out by Böttger and Tschirnhaus. The flowers and leaf sprigs applied on these white porcelains, such as on tankards, were, as on their Chinese counterparts, the main decorations. A number of polychrome and blue and white tankards with silver or pewter lids were made with Chinoiserie

An 18th century Chantilly bell-shaped mug, circa 1745. *Photograph: Christie's*

Porcelain bell-shaped mug with fluted loop handle, painted in iron red with a rim decoration made of gilt half-moons. Made at the Plymouth factory circa 1770. *Photograph: Christie's*

Derby mugs showing the influence of Sèvre in the painting of panels reserved on coloured grounds. The mug on the right is about 1795 with a free-standing bunch of flowers within a simple oval on a blue ground. On the left is a style typical of the Derby Regency period with flowers on a marble ledge in a gilded panel on a blue ground and is circa 1810.

A Derby cylindrical mug with a picture of St. Albans in a decorative panel, 4½ inches, made 1810-1825. *Photograph: Phillips*

scenes and some had porcelain covers, though very few have survived. The tankard with considerable open space provided ample opportunities for the excellent painted decoration for which Meissen is so well known. Their most famous decorator was J. G. Herold. He brought to the peak of achievement the decoration of flat unmoulded surfaces and developed a style that, although imitative of the Chinese, became essentially European.

In France, soon after Meissen was established, factories at St Cloud, Vincennes, Chantilly and Mennecy were leading the way to a highly successful tradition of soft-paste porcelain. Tankards and mugs were made, but as the French are traditionally wine and not ale drinkers, these were possibly made for export to ale-drinking countries such as Germany, Holland and England. The early white porcelain of St Cloud had a smooth creamy texture, richly decorated, in relief with fruit, flowers and leaf designs, the surface reeded and scaled in shapes influenced by silver engraving.

One of the most popular styles of decoration adopted by the Europeans from Japan was the 'kakiemon', the nickname of a potter from the Arita province who is alleged to have created it. Kakiemon design is characterized by the tasteful arrangement of

Two Derby head mugs of Jupiter and Neptune, late 18th or early 19th century. *Photograph: Phillips*

Left: Polychrome Bow porcelain mug with flared base and fluted loop handle, enamelled with chrysanthemums issuing from rockwork in Oriental style, circa 1752.
Middle: Polychrome bellshaped Bow tankard with original cover and remmants of a bird on top, circa 1760. Many bell-shaped porcelain mugs probably originally had lids as the intention was to copy silver tankards.
Right: Blue and white Bow mug of flared form with loop handle, painted with trees and flowers issuing from rockwork, circa 1775.

pictures of flowering shrubs, long-tailed birds, dragons, tigers and quails or partridges against large areas of undecorated white porcelain. Kakiemon is famous for an iron-red, but other common colours are blue, yellow and green. Meissen, St Cloud, Chantilly, Chelsea, Worcester and Bow enthusiastically copied the simple, elegant designs and kakiemon decoration often appears on mugs and tankards from these factories.

The difference between the hard-paste porcelain of China and Meissen, and the soft-pastes of early French factories and most of the English products, is essentially self-explanatory. The first is relatively cold and hard to the eye and touch, and the latter softer and more mellow, as the enamel colour tended to sink into the soft-paste glazes. However, for so long did the ceramics factories of England, the continent and America compete to invent the most superlative ceramic bodies, that various degrees of hardness were achieved and collectors of porcelain tend to develop their own strong preferences for certain types.

At Bristol (*c.* 1770–1781), Plymouth (*c.* 1768–1770) and New Hall (*c.* 1781–1835), hard porcelains were developed, but, as the dates show, the first two were short-lived and at New Hall hard-paste was made during only part of its history.

The Bristol factory known for true hard-paste porcelain was an off-shoot of Plymouth and both produced wares with numerous faults. However, they made many very fine pieces, and a mug from either would provide a rare example of the earliest hard-paste porcelain made in this country. The Bristol factory was noted for Chinese-style designs and attractive flower painting in a cottage style, and for leaf-green and red colours. It was also influenced by the more elaborate Sèvres styles.

The hard-paste Bristol factory is not to be confused with the Bristol Lund factory of *c.* 1750 that was later taken over by Worcester. Plymouth wares are distinguished by an inky-black tone to the underglaze blue chinese-style decoration.

Although longer-lived, the Chelsea factory's (1745–1769) useful wares such as mugs and tankards are as difficult to find as those

Bow bell-shaped mug enamelled in Oriental style with flowering chrysanthemums issuing from pierced rockwork with floral and trellis rim. *Photograph: Christie's*

A Bow cylindrical porcelain mug painted in underglaze blue with dragon motif, circa 1760-5, 4½ inches. *Photograph: Geoffrey Godden, chinaman*

of Plymouth and Bristol, simply because Chelsea is generally considered to be the earliest English porcelain factory and the best, so that items that have not been broken are already residing in private collections. The soft milky translucent body of the triangle-mark period was used to imitate silver forms, as well as Chinese and Meissen designs. Until 1771 the manager of the factory was Nicholas Sprimont, a former silversmith. Following the triangle period, the marks are chronologically known as the raised, red and gold anchor periods, the latter showing the influence of the lavishly decorated and gilded Sèvres porcelains.

At the Derby factory (*c.* 1750 to the present) the influence of Meissen was so great that it liked to be known as a 'second Dresden'. Intentions were, however, greater than fulfilment, for the soft-paste was rather chalky, the glaze tinged with blue and the figures clumsily modelled by comparison with Meissen. In the late 18th and early years of the 19th centuries the factory produced delicately painted wares on a warm body, and mellow-white glaze. Even in the later Bloor-Derby period (c. 1811–1826) high-quality painting was carried out. The factory made face mugs as a novelty, which are reminiscent of pottery Toby Jugs and the much later Martinware mugs and jugs. Before the Regency period flowers were painted free-standing in simple ovals on coloured grounds, but later on, during the Regency period itself, they were typically placed on a marble ledge.

Blue and white Chinese-influenced mugs and tankards of the 18th century are common among the porcelain factories where this form of decoration was much-loved, e.g. Worcester, Bow, Lowestoft, Caughley and Liverpool. The designs follow the Chinese originals more faithfully than many Europeanised Chinese motifs. Characteristic are the Chinese river scenes. The ubiquitous willow pattern in which a willow tree is prominent came late in the century – from about 1780 onwards – and arose more from the English imagination than the Chinese.

The Bow factory was the pioneer in England of blue and white

A rare matching pair of bell-shaped Worcester blue and white porcelain mugs, circa 1760, 5¾ inches high, showing Chinese-type decoration. *Photograph: Geoffrey Godden, chinaman*

A Caughley porcelain mug with the popular blue-printed Fisherman design, circa 1780, 4¾ inches. *Photograph: Geoffrey Godden, chinaman*

painted and transfer-printed wares in the Chinese manner. Robert Hancock, who later made Worcester famous for transfer-printing, is thought to have worked at Bow. Kakiemon designs were also popular at the factory. The famous partridges (or quails) appeared frequently on Bow, as well as other continental and English vessels. Bow, of which little is marked, was also noted for the applied prunus sprigs found on early wares.

A very high proportion (about 75 percent)[1] of Caughley or

[1] *British Porcelain*, Geoffrey Godden, Barrie & Jenkins, p. 86.

'Salopian' wares were painted or printed in underglaze blue in the Chinese manner. Other types of wares were blue and white with embellishments of gilding, and polychrome Chinese figures and flowers. Later decoration includes a type of Chantilly sprig pattern.

A number of antique mugs are found on the market made by Worcester and Royal Worcester, the firm with the longest continuous history of porcelain-manufacturing in this country.

A Caughley (left) and a Worcester (right) mug from the Geoffrey Godden collection, both printed in underglaze blue with each factory's version of the Fisherman pattern. This design was at one time thought only to be Caughley but the much finer Worcester version was found in great quantites on the Warmstry House site. The main differences between the two are that the Worcester fishing line wiggles while the Caughley line is straight and the Worcester fish is long and thin, while the Caughley fish is short and fat. They were made in the period 1776-1793.

Worcester Dr. Wall (1751-1783) cylindrical mug with fluted loop handle. The body is painted with floral swags suspended from gilt scrolls; the border decorations are blue and gilt. *Photograph: Christie's*

Much of the production of the Worcester factory has in the past been wrongly attributed to Caughley. This error was due to the attribution of the disguised Chinese numeral marks (the numbers 1–9 with strange Chinese-like squiggles through them) to Caughley, whereas these markings have now been found at Worcester excavation sites.

It used to be said also that one test of 18th-century Worcester was that it showed a green translucency by transmitted light, but wasters at the Worcester excavation site showed the orange translucency that used to be said was proof of Caughley. No longer can it be said that Worcester has a wiped-away glaze-free area on the inside of the footring. This very often appears on Worcester porcelains made *c.* 1760–1790, but it also is found on Caughley and Liverpool. And the underglaze violet-blue colour once attributed to Caughley is now believed to be Worcester. Discoveries too have been made concerning the famous 'fisherman' pattern, once held to be Caughley, but now attributable to both factories. The Worcester fishing-line wiggles, and the fish is long and thin, whereas the Caughley fish is short and fat and the fishing line straight.

Worcester took over Lund's Bristol works in 1752, although it was itself established in 1751. Both the Bristol and Worcester porcelains (and Caughley) were made of a soapstone body, and they were similar in other ways too, so that certain pieces once attributed to Bristol are now thought to be Worcester. The Worcester porcelains of the 18th century were a great achievement in terms of the body and the decoration: they were strong and practical while still being capable of being thinly potted and attractively coloured. The factory produced superb relief-moulded wares, well-painted underglaze blue Oriental designs and transfer-printed wares of very high quality. Even more famous were its scale-blue and other richly coloured grounds, with reserve panels of painted floral, bird and other designs. The term 'scale-blue' refers to the overlapping scales of colour.

A Coalport porcelain mug of about 1815 printed in underglaze-blue in the Chinese style, $3\frac{1}{4}$ inches high. *Photograph: Geoffrey Godden, chinaman*

Right: A Coalport mug inscribed in gilt "Success to the L.W.V." First quarter 19th century. *Photograph: Phillips*

The typical bell-shaped mug was followed by the generally later straight-sided cylindrical mug. Many Worcester mugs were made in blue and white Chinoiserie designs or floral patterns. The beautiful and justifiably famous Worcester apple-green ground colour is seen on the bell-shaped mug on the dust cover.

Mug collectors could confine themselves entirely to blue and white and still acquire a huge collection, made up of innumerable transfer-prints, painted decorations and examples from each factory. Spode, for instance, used at least 74 different transfers, although most appeared on their earthenwares. Spode was a great mass-producer, and by 1833 5,500 patterns had been used and many others were introduced thereafter. It was the second Josiah Spode (1755–1827) who introduced the now-famous English bone china in which hardy finely-potted tea-wares have been made ever since.

Longton Hall (c. 1750–1760) was a short-lived factory in Staffordshire which produced porcelain in the midst of a dense pottery area, and it therefore stands to reason that early porcelain that is similar to Staffordshire pottery models may well be from Longton Hall. In mugs and tankards, however, the shapes are very much the same as those of other porcelain manufacturers – bell-shaped, in-curving, tapering, and straight-sided cylindrical. Early straight-sided tankards were moulded with floral and scroll reserves based on silver patterns. Early mugs and tankards were thickly potted. Glazed bases are usual but there are some mugs with flat, unglazed bases. One fluted tapered mug was made decorated in colours with birds and flowers.

J. Sadler, who is mentioned in the chapter on pottery as having invented transfer-printing on ceramics (although some authorities say it began in Battersea a few years before in 1753), printed on Longton Hall porcelain. While at one time it was believed that these printed wares were products of the Liverpool porcelain-makers, it is now thought that the Liverpool makers were not making well-potted mugs suitable for overglaze printing, except for the Chaffers' factory, and that Sadler had bought plain mugs from Longton Hall and others, decorated them and sold them in Liverpool – from where, since it was a port and a major distribution centre for Staffordshire wares, they were sent far and wide.

Chinese patterns were common and many of the 40-some blue and white patterns were painted in a rapid freehand. Polychrome designs were often carelessly painted in the late years of the

A set of three early Minton porcelain mugs circa 1810 of a type often attributed to the Pinxton factory which issued similar designs, 6 inches and 4½ inches high. *Photograph: Geoffrey Godden, chinaman*

A relief-moulded Lowestoft porcelain cider mug painted in underglaze-blue, circa 1760, 4 inches high. *Photograph: Geoffrey Godden, chinaman*

factory. A number of tall cylindrical mugs with double scroll handles were made during the late period.

Many of the transfers on Longton Hall mugs depict heroes of the Seven Years' War (1756–1763); others bear the arms of societies such as the Foresters and the Society of Bucks, or family crests. Bonnie Prince Charlie is also commemorated. Most Longton Hall is unmarked.

John Ridgway (c. 1808–1855) specialized in bone-china table wares, including a number of bell-shaped and cylindrical mugs. Some are marked or can be identified by reference to the system of pattern-numbering set up at the factory, but many unmarked specimens have been wrongly attributed to other more fashionable factories, such as Rockingham.

Although the bone-china manufacturers of the 19th century provide more for the tea- and coffee-cup collector than the mug collector, they did supply a certain number of mugs. Rockingham, for instance, which of course made many pottery mugs, produced decorative porcelain mugs in some quantity. Examples are known bearing Wellington's portrait, probably made in 1828 when he became Prime Minister; and other personalities were probably also commemorated. There are also a certain number of mugs to be found with fine flower and scenic paintings and decorative gilding; others have a handle representing a horse's hoof and tail.

The Davernport firm (*c.* 1793–1887) at Longport, Staffordshire, also made both pottery and porcelain. Very little is known about the pre-1830 porcelain, but the post-1830 work was similar in style to that of Coalport. However, there were a number of commemorative and souvenir mugs in Davenport porcelain, with transfer-printed scenes and pictures: among the subjects are Lichfield and Gloucester Cathedrals, Boscombe House, St Peter's Collegiate Church (Wolverhampton), St Mary's School Birkenhead, and the 'Primitive Methodist Jubillee Chapel Tunstall', dated 1860. The joint founders of the Primitive Methodists, Hugh Bourne and William Clowes, are also commemorated. The preoccupation with the sect may be due to the fact that Clowes is

A Lowestoft porcelain presentation mug of bell shape painted in underglaze blue, 1768, 5¾ inches high. *Photograph: Geoffrey Godden, chinaman*

Modern Coalport mug commemorating restoration work on the Ironbridge over the River Severn. It is decorated with a print of the bridge and surrounding countryside in pink on white fine bone china with gold bands encircling the rim and base and a leaf design in relief with gold on the handle. This is a copy of a piece originally produced by Coalport at the beginning of the 19th century commemorating the building of the bridge in 1779. It was made in a limited edition of 1779 and cost £5·50 in 1972. *Photograph: Coalport*

said to have served an apprenticeship at the Davenport works and to have been one of Major John Davenport's Volunteers during the French wars.

Coalport has had a long and distinguished history of porcelain-manufacturing from c. 1796 to the present day. Early pieces are unmarked and are sometimes mistakenly attributed to Worcester or New Hall. The early body is a type of hard-paste which is thickly potted and feels heavy.

Before establishing the Coalport factory, John Rose was apprenticed to Thomas Turner at Caughley. He then took over the Caughley Works in 1799. The firm made underglaze-blue Chinese-style printed mugs, and produced commemorative mugs early in its history. The company is now part of the Wedgwood group, and continues to make commemoratives.

New Hall was the second major Staffordshire firm after Longton Hall to make porcelain in that area, and it is the only other firm to have made English hard-paste like that of Bristol and Plymouth. There is considerable dispute as to what products were made at New Hall and which should be attributed to Caughley, Coalport, Minton or Chamberlain.

Minton and Pinxton issued mugs bearing similar scenic designs, but, whereas Pinxton folded in 1813, Minton's went on to produce porcelain of extremely fine quality during the

1850–1900 period, in particular between 1860 and 1880. It is still making porcelain to this day.

Lowestoft (1757–1799) was responsible for a number of mugs catering for local markets around the Suffolk coast. Designs are broadly based on Chinese designs and, until the early 1770s, all the decoration was in underglaze-blue. In that decade the Oriental fashion for underglaze-blue to be used in conjunction with overglaze enamels of reds, greens and some gilding, is seen on Lowestoft. There were a number of mugs made on commission for individuals, bearing personal names, inscriptions and dates. Lowestoft mugs inscribed 'A Trifle from Bungay' and other local places are popular enough to have been reproduced in continental hard-paste porcelain.

A great deal of snobbery, both academic and prejudiced, exists among collectors of porcelain, which does not affect pottery, pewter, glass or even silver. Endless verbal and written debates and discourses are carried on to prove attributions to

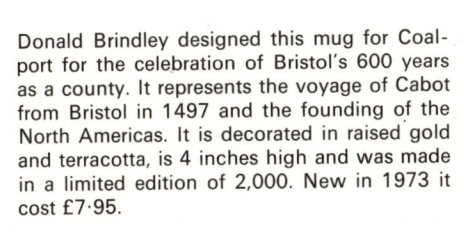

Donald Brindley designed this mug for Coalport for the celebration of Bristol's 600 years as a county. It represents the voyage of Cabot from Bristol in 1497 and the founding of the North Americas. It is decorated in raised gold and terracotta, is 4 inches high and was made in a limited edition of 2,000. New in 1973 it cost £7·95.

Superb example of the flowering shrubs and long-tailed birds characteristic of English Kakiemon-style porcelain. This is a particularly rare example as it was made by William Ball's Factory in Liverpool circa 1755-60. *Photograph: Winifred Williams*

this or that factory. Fortunately, the mug or tankard collector does not have to worry too much about marks or their absence, since mugs – more common by far than tankards – are probably of least interest to porcelain collectors as they do not reflect the 'refined' shapes of figures, vases, tureens, plates and tea cups for which the material is best-known.

No such problems exist in any case with modern porcelain mugs, as they are generally marked with makers' names. Modern porcelain commemorative mugs have proved a successful line for famous firms such as Coalport, Wedgwood and Worcester, because the strength of their reputations for high quality, combined with the need people seem to feel to slow down the course of history by stopping to mark events, have created ready markets. Commemoratives provide an excuse for fans of a particular factory, or of the personality or event being immortalized, to buy the product.

Chapter Six
GLASS, LEATHER AND WOOD

Glass brought a lightness and grace to the mug and tankard such as no other material could. Not only does the plasticity of molten glass allow it to be coaxed into slim, fragile shapes, but the material lends itself superbly to being engraved and cut, adding a new element of movement and sparkle. Glass is today relatively inexpensive, and is commonly used in the making of beer mugs, but in pre-Victorian times, when there were glass taxes in force, it was used more for the smallest and most delicate of drinking vessels.

Glass in its simplest form is sand and ashes. It is made by fusing silica or sand with an alkali of soda or potash at high temperature. In its simplest form it has a green or blue colour, caused by the iron in the sand.

Crystal clarity is achieved by introducing certain oxides, notably manganese dioxide, which neutralize the iron present. The Romans were familiar with this process.

When the Romans conquered Britain in the first century AD, the glass industry was already at least 3000 years old and extremely advanced. A technique of glass blowing had been invented, probably in Syria a century before, and glass could be mass-produced.

Roman glass was made with a soda alkali derived from sea plants or soda from the Egyptian desert. This sea plant was imported into Gaul, the Rhineland and Britain to make soda glass almost up to 1000 AD.

Engraving techniques were still relatively undeveloped however. The Romans engraved by hand with flints, without the aid of a wheel, and – as they were virtually digging into a hard surface – they produced jagged lines. Some experts believe the Romans engraved merely to make an outline to be traced later with enamel paint, which has since worn off.

17th century mug of colourless lead glass made in London, probably by Ravenscroft's Savoy Glass House. *Photograph: London Museum.*

Gradually the source of soda from the Mediterranean dried up and European glasshouses switched to potash, derived from woodland plants, as an alkali. This 'forest glass' as it was known was common until Venetian glassmakers came to London in the 15th and 16th centuries, and began making the famous Venetian styles.

Venetian glass reigned supreme in the world during the 16th century and Europe competed for the services of Venetian makers. Their glass, thin and delicate but ductile, was more workable than the English lead glass that followed.

The first known party of Venetians came to London about 1547, led by Iseppo Casseler. They set up the first recorded glasshouse in London in Aldgate, and continued making drinking glasses there until 1569. At this time, in Tudor England, glass was valued to the same degree as, and sometimes more than, precious stones and metals.

The greatest name in English glassmaking during the 16th century was Jacob Verzelini, Venice-born, but a resident of Belgium before he came to England. He secured a monopoly of 21 years from the crown for making 'Venice glasses' from 1575.

The next great monopoly extended to all glassmaking in Great Britain and lasted until 1656. This was secured by Sir Robert Mansell who had glasshouses in the City, Southwark,

A Ravenscroft mug or jug of c. 1680 showing the crizzling problem that affected flint glass before lead was added to the process. The bulbous body and cylindrical neck are similar to certain silver and earthenware shapes of the day.

Lambeth and Greenwich as well as all over the country.

From 1660 onwards, the Glass Sellers' Company led a drive to improve the industry which culminated in Ravenscroft's new lead crystal.

Late 17th century or early 18th century English glass mug of walsted shape with coin design in knop, applied rings of glass around the rim and diamond pattern around the base. *Photograph: Richard Dennis.*

117

Glass mug from the second half of the 18th century with applied rings of glass around the rim and gadrooning around the base. *Photograph: Richard Dennis.*

George Ravenscroft was a chemist who was to develop flint and then lead crystal that would put England in the forefront of glass manufacture by the end of the 17th century. This crystal was a material tougher than Venetian soda glass. At first, due to an excess of alkali, the flint glass crizzled or clouded due to a large number of minute cracks, but eventually glass with lead was perfected and English glasshouses proliferated.

At one time in England there were 30 glasshouses – nine of them in London – making lead glass, and glass vied with pottery as one of the leading industries.

Ravenscroft sealed many of his products with the Raven's Head, but the practice of marking glass unfortunately never became widespread.

The evidence for dating glass is slim compared with that for ceramics, silver and gold, so commemorative glass is often popular with collectors because it records an event and often the date.

A glass mug engraved with hops and barley above the name "H. Hinde," 7⅜ inches, mid-18th century. The hops and barley motif, clearly identifying the mug with the consumption of ale, continued to be used during the next 100 years or so. The applied trailed glass below the rim and diamond moulding around the base are characteristic features. *Photograph: Phillips*

In tableware English lead glass was heavier and more durable than Venetian soda glass. It was also less plastic, but what it lost in suitability for moulded ornaments and serpent stems, it gained in light-refracting qualities, simple, robust designs, and fine proportions.

The Glass Excise Act of 1745–6 however forced English glass design towards lighter and more slender proportions, as tax was imposed on glass by weight. The tax coincided with the Georgian taste for elegance, which reinforced the demand for lighter glass.

18th century free-blown glass mugs of typical waisted shape, with applied rings of glass under the rim, gadrooning around the bases, and strong foot-rings. *Photographs: W. G. T. Burne*

18th century free-blown glass mugs based on silver shapes. *Photograph: W. G. T. Burne*

Glass-cutting became an English and Irish speciality in the later part of the 18th century, and continued to be important through Victorian times when cutting became increasingly ostentatious, particularly after the repeal of the Glass Excise Act in 1845.

Fancy multi-coloured glass became popular among many Victorians, while others were drawn to the new shapes and delicate colours inspired by William Morris.

The making of glass mugs would appear to date from the late 17th century, when the English glass industry was given a strong push forward with the invention and perfection of lead glass by Ravenscroft between 1673 and 1675. This was noted for its brilliance and strength, and its popularity soon spread to other parts of Europe. The superlative new glass enabled all manner of new

Glass mug $4\frac{1}{2}$ inches high, circa 1740, English, with gadrooning around base and applied rings of glass under the rim to enrich. *Photograph: Phillips*

objects to be made, and certainly by the early 18th century the glass mug was well-established. However, they were probably not very popular, Pewter and stoneware mugs were commonly employed for holding small beer and cider, and ale glasses and the heavy drinking glasses known as rummers were also used for ale. Since they usually had large capacious bowls, rummers were probably in use in taverns, inns and pubs for holding beer, ale, cider and sack in the 19th century until they were gradually succeeded by the modern beer mug after pressed glass was introduced about 1840 and the Glass Excise Tax was lifted in 1845. This was the time when pewter, traditionally the most popular tavern container for beer, was becoming more highly valued, and many pewter mugs and tankards were being stolen. As they were expensive to replace, and because there had been incidents of lead poisoning, the use of pewter more or less died out by the turn of the century except where mugs were reserved for personal use.

Engraved glass mug of the late 18th century, with hops and barley motif.

Late 18th century glass simulating a barrel with binding hoops and of a type found also in silver, pewter and pottery. Photograph: Richard Dennis

After 1714 glass mugs were available with thick solid feet and substantial handles. However, most glasses were stemmed; and after the 1745–46 Glass Excise Act especially, heavy, sturdy examples would have become very expensive. Duty was payable at 9s. 4d. per hundredweight of new glass, but as this did not apply to old broken glass, makers encouraged their clientele to turn in their old for new, thus bringing about the destruction of many examples of the older styles.

Despite the taxes, however, it should be emphasised that glass was greatly admired and valued and those who could afford it took great pride in having it in their homes.

Beer mugs were made throughout the 18th century, sometimes engraved with hops and barley, sometimes with apples if they were intended to hold cider, sometimes with a name or date. At the base was often gadrooning or a diamond moulding; and just below the rim there might be thin lines of applied trailed glass. The most usual shape was slightly waisted.

Bohemia has a tradition of glass-making that stretches from the 14th century, when glass refining was developed, to the present day, when hand-engraving is still a living art form in Czechoslovakia. In about 1600 there were numerous artisans cutting precious and semi-precious stones for the Emperor of Bohemia, Rudolph II. Soon, with rock crystal always relatively scarce, the cutters turned to crystal glass. By the end of the 17th century, a transparent, lustrous glass very like rock crystal was being used; and a lime-glass had been developed that was even more brilliant and lent itself superbly to contrast with the matt finish left by the engraver's tools.

Engraved glass was in great demand at the end of the 17th century and beginning of the 18th. Mugs and tankards, glasses and beakers were prepared for journeymen who travelled from place to place to engrave on personal request coats of arms, initials, landscapes, framed medallions, ornamental lacework, birds, fantastic animals, bouquets of flowers, hunting scenes, representations of the continents, seasons and senses, and whatever other motifs were desired. Mugs and tankards were made as commemorative items to mark an event or to serve as souvenirs of cities, castles, abbeys, convents and spas.

During the 19th century a great deal of mass-produced Bohemian glass found its way in the form of souvenir and fairground mugs both to Germany and England. These mugs were

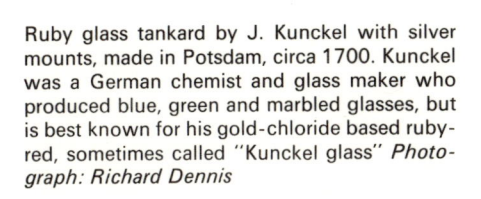

Ruby glass tankard by J. Kunckel with silver mounts, made in Potsdam, circa 1700. Kunckel was a German chemist and glass maker who produced blue, green and marbled glasses, but is best known for his gold-chloride based ruby-red, sometimes called "Kunckel glass" *Photograph: Richard Dennis*

often made in coloured glass, such as amber, amethyst and ruby, and painted with flowers and inscriptions such as 'A present from Margate'.

Another type of glass, made in Bohemia and throughout Europe, imitated the new porcelain developed first at Meissen. This was opaque-white or milk glass ('Milchglas'). Decoration was similar to that on porcelain, with Chinoiserie themes favoured, as well as scenes after Watteau, mythological subjects and genre scenes.

Later, in the 19th century, opaline glass, which is semi-transparent, was also made in imitation of porcelain, in France and England.

One of the leading glassmaking centres of the 18th century was Bristol. By 1725, there were about 15 glasshouses in the area. Being a port, Bristol was in a favoured position both for the import of raw materials and for the distribution of English glass, clear (lead) glass and coloured, to other parts of the country and abroad. There was also an abundance of the necessary raw materials in the area.

Bohemian tankard three-colour layer glass of clear, white and pink, also painted and gilded, circa 1840. *Photograph: Richard Dennis.*

Bristol has been given credit for the opaque-white glass mugs, and other types decorated in enamel colours with motifs of flowers, birds and Chinese figures as on porcelain, though in fact it was made in other parts of the country as well. This type of decoration was inspired not only by the wish to jump on to the bandwagon of the new European porcelain, but by the fact that this kind of glass was not taxed until 1777, and so enjoyed 32 years' advantage over other glasses.

The now-famous Bristol blue which so excites collectors was probably made at other centres besides Bristol, such as Newcastle, London and Stourbridge. Besides the rich blue, there was a paler blue, as well as amethyst, green and sometimes red. Very little is signed and that which is will probably bear the name 'J. Jacobs, Bristol'. These may have been decorated by Lazarus Jacobs or his son Jacob, or by Michael Edkins, another decorator in the city, who is known to have done work for the Jacobs. In the early 19th century, Bristol coloured glass appealed to a less elite clientele, who demanded souvenirs bearing slogans to indicate where the mug or tankard came from.

Nailsea glass is another category the origins of which are not certain. Allegedly made near Bristol at the Nailsea Glass Works, the coloured, fanciful glass, for which there was a great vogue in the 19th century due to demand from sailors and tourists, was in fact made at a number of centres in the country. The Nailsea glassworks (1788–1873) made items of bottle glass in dark brown, dark green or smoky green, and then decorated them with (mainly white) enamel, fused-on in flecks, threads, loops and stripes. This they did to avoid the heavy duty imposed on glass by the

Mass-produced in Bohemia during the third quarter of the 19th century for the English fairground and souvenir market, these coloured glass mugs are from left to right amber, amethyst, and ruby. They are hand-painted and hand-blown and still inexpensive to collect. *Photograph: Richard Dennis*

125

18th century Bohemian milk glass mug and tankard with painted enamel decoration. *Photograph: Richard Dennis.*

Glass Excise Acts, as bottle glass was not taxed so severely. But the firm also made items in lead glass, clear or pale green, with latticinio, or combed-glass decoration, in colours.

The duties on glass, combined with the establishment of free trade with Ireland in 1780, encouraged an exodus of English glass-makers to Ireland where luxurious cut-glass mugs were made in the opulent Regency taste. As the tax was imposed on the weight of the material before any was cut away, cutters in England tended to use shallow cutting techniques such as fluting.

Cut glass has been popular off and on since Roman days, since cutting shows off so effectively the light-refractory qualities of the material, particularly of lead glass which contains such sparkle or 'fire'.

At about the time of the popularisation of Bohemian glass

came competition from the American blown-three-mould and pressed glass industries, which had developed in an attempt to provide a cheap alternative to the very popular but expensive Irish and English cut glass. The technique of blowing molten glass into moulds of two, three or four sections (but mostly three: hence the name) was popular between about 1820–1830 in America and was essentially a means of mass-production. It did nevertheless, entail skilled finishing off by hand.

Machine-pressed glass came in about 1825 and eventually superseded the blown-three-mould technique. By 1829, it was being produced on a large commercial scale at the Sandwich Glass factory in Sandwich, Massachusetts. The process involved pouring glass into a patterned mould, then pressing a plunger manually or mechanically into the glass, spreading it to all parts of the pattern. The plunger, being smooth, left the inside of the vessel without impressions from the mould on the outside, whereas in the blown-three-mould system the pattern of the mould shows on the inside as well as the out. The 'lacy pattern' much loved in American pressed glass was a finely stippled, lace-like background designed to bring sparkle to the dull surface of moulded glass.

At the same time as these two industrial techniques provided inexpensive glass for the table, cut glass in the Irish and English manner was also being made at a number of American glass-houses, reaching a peak of popularity in about 1880 when many families were able to afford at least a few items. They were

Early 19th century Nailsea glass mug. *Photograph: Richard Dennis.*

American mug with applied threads dating from the late 18th century in a style made known in southern New Jersey. Shown with other American glass from the Corning Museum of Glass, New York. *Photograph: Loaned by Walter Parrish International. Reproduced by permission Corning Museum of Glass, Corning, New York.*

extremely popular as wedding presents.

Earlier and less mechanical techniques were, of course, also employed by glasshouses in America. Free-blown glass was made as well as pattern-moulded ware. The latter was the forerunner of blown-three-mould glass, being a method of achieving a pattern on glass by blowing it into small moulds and then enlarging the object by further free-blowing and, finally finishing off by hand.

Henry William Stiegel went from Germany to America in 1750 and founded a glassworks named after him where free-blown, engraved and enamelled glass was produced. Many glasses were of rich colours, such as purple, amethyst, blue and, more rarely, emerald green. Stiegel's firm was also responsible for a number of items engraved or enamelled with German folk motifs.

The most successful American glass-house of the 18th century was that established in 1739 by Caspar Wistar, a German, in southern New Jersey. Although engaged in the large-scale commercial production of bottles and window glass, the firm set up a corner for the personal use of the blowers who made a great many decorative and useful pieces for their friends and families. Free-blown and hand-manipulated items were made and decorated with 'lily-pad' patterns, applied prunts and threading.

Pressed glass quickly spread to England and France, and by about 1840 all manner of tablewares were being produced in imitation of cut glass in England, where the same patterns continued to be used for the next 50 years. Much English pressed glass came from the Sunderland and Newcastle area. Although not a very respectable subject for collection at the moment, doubtless pressed glass, which is so very inexpensive now, will in due course attract loving supporters. Already commemorative, and to a lesser extent souvenir, pressed glass – for which the system was most usefully applied – is being collected and housed with older and more respected commemorative items.

Cut and pressed glass can be readily distinguished because the latter has more regular, less sharp facets than true cut glass, and it also of course shows less refracted brilliance. If the mould seams have not been polished away, as they often were on the better pieces, these are also tell-tale signs.

The lifting of the glass tax in 1845 enabled manufacturers to respond to the love of show among Victorian middle classes with even greater extravagences of form and colour. Colour was

American pattern-moulded mug and beaker, probably made at the Stiegel glassworks of Henry William Stiegel about 1765-1774. He is thought to have made wares enameled and engraved with typical German folk motifs for sale to his Pennsylvania Dutch neighbours as well as more sophisticated pattern-moulded wares for the seaboard cities. Corning Museum of Glass, New York. *Photograph: Loaned by Walter Parrish International. Reproduced by permission Corning Museum of Glass, Corning, New York.*

American cut glass mug showing the Anglo-Irish influences on Eastern American glassmakers. It was probably made at the Union Flint Glass Works in Kensington, near Philadelphia about 1826-1840. In the Corning Museum of Glass, New York. *Photograph: Loaned by Walter Parrish International. Reproduced by permission Corning Museum of Glass, Corning, New York.*

achieved by adding metallic oxides to the molten liquid, by staining or painting, by adding layers of coloured glass to the clear and then cutting sections away. There were sophisticated circles who demanded high-quality engraved, cut and colourless glass, as well as more tasteless circles who appreciated gaudiness and novelty.

The black-jack is a romantic vessel to those who dream of Jacobean and Stuart times, of rollicking dinners on stout oak tables; or even of earlier days when the leather bottle was used to drink from by peasants and barons alike, in taverns or in the pastures, when riding with the hounds or entertaining in the baronial hall.

Made in various sizes the black-jack was a bottle-shaped tankard, pewter-lined and embellished with silver mounts. Leather tankards of cylindrical shape were also made. The leather is tanned and then soaked in cold water until fully impregnated. The water is them 'sammed' or drained off, leaving the leather soft and plastic. After this, it can be moulded or shaped by using moulds, dies or presses.

The following is a record of some of the wooden and leather drinking vessels, including mugs ('Kannes') tankards and black-jacks, in use in 1635:

Of drinking cups divers and sundry sorts we have; some of elme, some of box, some of maple, some of holly, etc.; mazers, broad-mouthed dishes, noggins, whiskins, piggins, crinzes, ale-bowls, wassell-bowls, court-dishes, tankards, kannes, from a pottle to a pint, from a pint to a gill. Other bottles we have of leather, but they are most used amongst shepheards and harvest-people of the countrey: small jacks we have in many ale-houses of the citie and suburbs, tip't with silver, besides the great black jacks and bombards at the court, which when the Frenchmen first saw, they reported, at their returne into their countrey, that the Englishmen used to drinke out of their bootes: we have, besides, cups made of hornes of beasts, of cocker-nuts, of goords, of the eggs of ostriches; others made of the shells of divers fishes, brought from the Indies and other places, shining like mother of pearle . . .[1]

[1] From *Heywood's Philocothonista* or *The Drunkard Opened* (1635), quoted in *Treen and Other Wooden Bygones* by Edward H. Pinto, G. Bell & Sons, p. 30.

Glass mug with an engraved ballooning theme, circa 1810-20. *Photograph: Richard Dennis.*

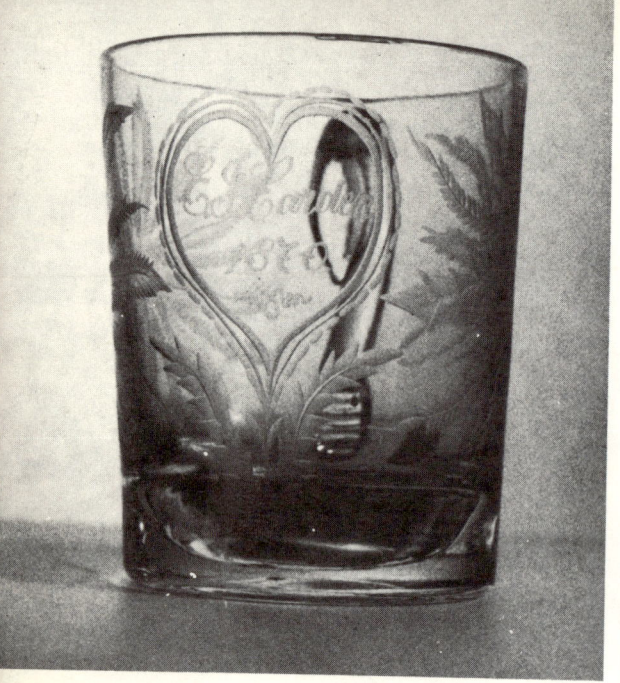

Above: Two views of a free-blown glass mug inscribed "E. J. Carden 1870." Possibly the mug was made about 30 years earlier. *Photograph: John Brooks*

Below: Two views of an example of commemorative pressed glass made for the opening of a bridge at Newcastle-on-Tyne in 1850. *Photograph: John Brooks*

Wooden tankards were in common use in homes and taverns by about 960 AD. But much earlier examples also exist. These are Celtic mugs (known as 'Celtic tankards') of about 50 BC to 50 AD made of wood, bronze and brass. One in the Merseyside County Museum is concave and over 7 inches in diameter, with a bronze handle of graceful scrolls, cast in trumpet pattern. It appears not to have had a lid, and, therefore, within the terminology of this book, comes under the category of a mug.

The peg tankard mentioned in the first and second chapters was originally a wooden vessel. King Edgar (944–977) in an attempt to decrease drunkenness ordained that drinking vessels should have pins or nails set in them so that any person who drank past the mark at one draught should have to pay a penny, half of which would go to the accuser and half to the town treasury. I dare say this scheme added to the town coffers and to personal vendettas against those who told on each other, but did little to combat drunkenness.

The tankards in question were of two-quart capacity, made of staves of oak or pine and usually bound with hoops of wattle.

Examples of English pressed glass from the second half of the 19th century. The third from the right, top row, has a VR seal in relief to guarantee pint capacity and is an indication that press-moulded glass was in use in pubs during Victorian times. *Photograph: Richard Dennis*

Left: Victorian slag glass mug of 1882, commemorating a world famous oarsman called Hanlin from Toronto. Slag glass was press-moulded in Gateshead and Sunderland and contained slag from the iron foundries. *Photograph: John Brooks*

Above right: A modern Toby jug of glass by Whitefriars.

Right: Leather-covered metal tankard decorated with Sheffield plate. Late 18th century. *Photograph: Walsall Museum, Walsall*

Most had wooden handles and lids and were lined with pitch.

Very few British or Irish wooden tankards have survived, and it is unlikely that many collectors will be lucky enough to acquire one. However, a great many were made into the 19th century in the heavily wooded countries of north-west Europe, such as Scandinavia, and examples of these one may come across from time to time. Edward Pinto wrote in *Treen and Other Wooden Bygones* that 'Wooden tankards were the commonest drinking vessels of North-west Europe over many centuries'.[2] They were often elaborately carved and have substantial covers and handles with large thumbpieces. In place of mugs, it appears that cups and bowls of wood were most commonly used for ale and beer.

[2] Ibid, pp 57–58.

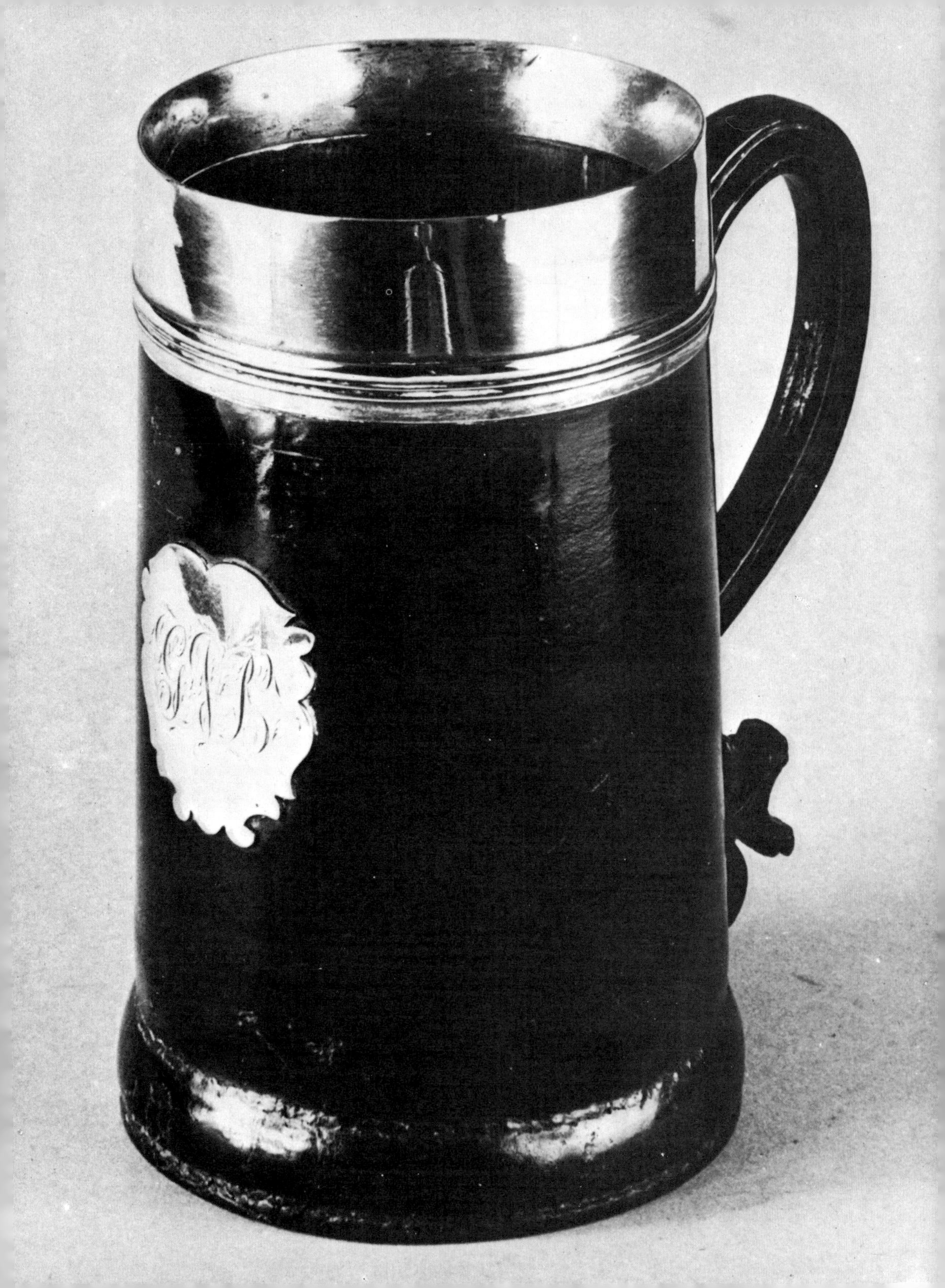

BIBLIOGRAPHY

Archer, Michael and Garner, F.H. ENGLISH DELFTWARE. London: Faber and Faber, 1972.

Ash, Douglas. DICTIONARY OF BRITISH ANTIQUE SILVER. London: Pelham Books, 1972.

Ash, Douglas. HOW TO IDENTIFY ENGLISH SILVER DRINKING VESSELS. 630–1830. London: G. Bell and Sons Ltd., 1964.

"Beer and Ale", COLLIER'S ENCYCLOPEDIA, Vol. 3. New York: P.F. Collier & Son Corporation, 1958.

Cameron, Ian and Kingsley-Rowe, Elizabeth, Editors. ENCYCLOPEDIA OF ANTIQUES. London & Glasgow: Collins, 1973.

Comstock, Helen, Editor. THE CONCISE ENCYCLOPEDIA OF AMERICAN ANTIQUES. New York: Hawthorn Books, Inc., 1969.

Cotterell, Howard Herschel, Riff, Adolphe and Vetter, Robert M. NATIONAL TYPES OF OLD PEWTER: A REVISED AND EXPANDED EDITION. Princeton: The Pyne Press, 1972. Republication of original material published by the Magazine ANTIQUES from 1927 to 1935.

Cotterell, Howard Herschel. PEWTER DOWN THE AGES. Plymouth: The Mayflower Press, 1932.

Du Cann, C.G.L. "Georgian Toby Jugs." London: ART AND ANTIQUES WEEKLY, Independent Magazines Ltd., April 5, 1975.

Eaglestone, Arthur A., and Lockett, T.A. THE ROCKINGHAM POTTERY: NEW REVISED EDITION. Newton Abbot: David and Charles, 1973.

Elville, E.M. THE COLLECTOR'S DICTIONARY OF GLASS. London: Country Life Ltd., 1961, reprinted 1965.

Godden, Geoffrey. BRITISH PORCELAIN: AN ILLUSTRATED GUIDE. London: Barrie & Jenkins Ltd., 1974.

Godden, Geoffrey. BRITISH POTTERY: AN ILLUSTRATED GUIDE. London: Barrie & Jenkins Ltd., 1974.

Godden, Geoffrey. THE ILLUSTRATED GUIDE TO RIDGWAY PORCELAINS. London: Barrie & Jenkins Ltd., 1972.

Harris, Ian. THE PRICE GUIDE TO ANTIQUE SILVER. Woodbridge: The Antique Collectors' Club, 1969.

Harris, Ian. THE PRICE GUIDE TO VICTORIAN SILVER. Woodbridge: The Antique Collectors' Club, 1971.

Haslam, Malcolm. POTTERY. London: Orbis Publishing Ltd., 1972.

Holgate, David. NEW HALL AND ITS IMITATORS. London: Faber and Faber, 1971.

Janes, Hurford. THE RED BARREL: A HISTORY OF WATNEY MANN. London: John Murray, 1963.

Lewis, Mel. "A Skinful." London: ART AND ANTIQUES WEEKLY' Independent Magazines Ltd., October 27, 1973.

Lloyd, Ward. INVESTING IN GEORGIAN GLASS. London: Barrie & Rockliff, The Cresset Press, 1969.

Lockett, T.A. DAVENPORT POTTERY AND PORCELAIN 1794-1887. Newton Abbot: David and Charles, 1972.

Mackay, James. COMMEMORATIVE POTTERY AND PORCELAIN. London: Garnstone Press, 1971.

Masse, H.J.L.J., and Michaelis, Ronald F. THE PEWTER COLLECTOR. London: Barrie & Jenkins Ltd., 1971.

May, John and Jennifer. COMMEMORATIVE POTTERY 1780-1900. London: Heinemann, 1972.

Michaelis, Ronald F. BRITISH PEWTER. London and Sydney: Ward Lock & Co. Ltd., 1969.

Monckton, H.A. "A Historical Survey of English Ale, Beer and Public Houses." London: BREWERS GUILD JOURNAL, Incorporated Brewers' Guild, September, 1968.

Morley-Fletcher, Hugo. MEISSEN. London: Barrie & Jenkins Ltd., 1971.

Oman, Charles. ENGLISH DOMESTIC SILVER. London: Adam and Charles Black, 1968.

Peal, Christopher A. BRITISH PEWTER AND BRITANNIA METAL FOR PLEASURE AND INVESTMENT. London: John Gifford, 1971.

Pěsatová, Zuzana. BOHEMIAN ENGRAVED GLASS. London: Paul Hamlyn, 1968.

Phelps, Warren. IRISH GLASS. London: Faber and Faber Ltd., 1970.

Phillips, Phoebe, Editor. THE COLLECTORS' ENCYCLOPEDIA OF ANTIQUES. London: THE CONNOISSEUR, 1973.

Pinto, Edward H. TREEN AND OTHER WOODEN BYGONES. London: G. Bell & Sons Ltd., 1969.

Reilly, Robin. WEDGWOOD JASPER. London: Charles Letts & Co. Ltd., 1972.

Rodgers, David. CORONATION SOUVENIRS AND COMMEMORATIVES. London: Latimer New Dimensions Ltd., 1975.

Sandon, Henry. THE ILLUSTRATED GUIDE TO WORCESTER PORCELAIN, 1751–1793. London: Herbert Jenkins, 1969.

Shelley, Roland J.A. "A Pewter Hammerhead Baluster Measure of circa 1530." London: *Apollo*, Apollo Magazine Ltd., June 1947.

Sykes, Christopher. "Welcome Signs." London: ART AND ANTIQUES WEEKLY, Independent Magazines Ltd., October 27, 1973.

Tait, Hugh. PORCELAIN. London, New York, Sydney, Toronto: Hamlyn, 1966.

Watney, Bernard. LONGTON HALL PORCELAIN. London: Faber and Faber, 1957.

Wills, Geoffrey. GLASS. London: Orbis Publishing, 1972.

INDEX

Adams, Samuel, 16
agate wares, 82
Alden, John, 14, 16
Alexandra, Princess, 70
Aller-Vale, 86
American glass, 127, 128, 129, 130
American pewter, 56, 57, 58
American pottery, 84, 85
American silver, 31, 32, 35
Amiens, Peace of, 66
animal mugs, 68, 72, 74, 75, 77
Anne, Princess, 65, 92
anti-wobble, 55
Aquinas Locke, 60
armorial silver, 36
art deco, 90, 91
art nouveau, 30, 86, 90
Ashberry, 44
Association of British Pewter Craftsmen, 58, 59, 60
Augustine, St., 10
Augustus the Strong, Elector of Saxony, 96
Ault, 86

baluster measures, 44, 46, 53, 54
Barlow, Hannah, 73, 74, 82
barrel shape, 75, 76, 84
basalt, 75, 76, 84

Bath, founding of, 63
beer:
   American, 14, 16
   bottled, 12
   small, 12, 14, 18
Belch, Sir Toby, 20, 70
Bennett, Edwin, 86
Benney, Gerald, 31, 34
Bernese flagon, 46, 55
Binsted, Arthur, 6, 13, 25
black jack, 130
blanc de Chine, 95, 96
blown-three-mould glass, 127, 128
Bohemian glass, 122, 123, 124, 126
bone China, 109, 110, 112
Boscombe House, 111
Boswell, 20
Bourne, Hugh, 111
Böttger, 96
Bow, 100, 102, 103, 104
brandy, 12
bride-ale, 11
Bristol Charter, 63, 113
Bristol glass, 124, 125
Bristol porcelain, 101, 102, 112
Bristol pottery, 66
Britannia metal, 44, 53
Britannia standard, 27, 35
Broadhead and Atkin, 44

139

Cade Designs, 60
Calverley, C. S., 17
cans or kannes, 18, 25, 30
Casseler, Iseppo, 116
Caughley, 103, 104, 106, 107, 112
Celtic "tankard", 18, 133
Chamberlain, 112
Chantilly, 96, 97, 99, 100, 105
Charles II, 25, 62
Charles, Prince of Wales, 65, 91
Chasing, 34
Chaucer, 20
Chelsea, 100, 102
Chichely, Robert, 42
children's mugs, 15, 21, 29, 31, 34, 68, 69, 72, 75, 76, 77
Chinese influence, 81, 93, 96, 99, 100, 101, 102, 103, 104, 105, 108, 124, 125
chopine, 53
christening mugs, 15, 21, 29, 34
Churchill, Winston, 63, 70
cider, 17, 21, 121, 122
Cliff, Clarice, 91
Colsman's Improved Compost, 44
Clowes, William, 111
Coalport, 107, 108, 111, 112, 113, 114
commemoratives:
  glass, 118, 123, 125, 129, 132, 134
  pewter, 40, 41
  porcelain, 111, 112, 114
  pottery, 61–68, 69, 70, 71, 73, 74

Royal, 62, 64, 65, 67, 68, 69, 91
silver, 29, 31, 33
creamware, 61, 75, 76, 80, 84, 86
Cromwell, 12, 62
"cut-card" decoration, 26, 27
cut glass, 120, 126, 127, 129, 130

Davenport, 87, 110, 111, 112
delft, English, 79, 80, 81, 82, 85
Derby, 98, 99, 102, 103
Devlin, Stuart, 31
Dickens, Charles, 63
Dixon and Smith, 44
Dixon and Sons, 44
Doccia, 96
Doulton, 72, 73, 82, 86
drinking song, 18

Ecbright, Archbishop of York, 10
Edgar the Peaceful, King of England, 10, 133
Edict of Nantes, 27
Edkins, Michael, 125
Edward I, 36, 42
Edward VII, 64, 70
Edward VIII, 64
Egypt, 9
Elizabeth II, Queen, 64
Elwes, Henry, 70
embossing, 34, 37
Englefields, 60
engraving, 23, 26, 34, 37, 115, 118, 119, 121, 122, 123, 124, 125, 128, 129, 130, 131, 132
"entire", 14

face and head mugs, 73, 81, 99, 103
fakes, 36, 69, 73
Farnham, 86
Fillpot, Toby, 70, 78
flagons, 12, 13, 31, 40, 41, 45, 46, 48, 52, 54, 55, 56
Float, Augustin, 25
Forester, Thomas, 91
Friendly Society, 65
frog mugs, 67, 68, 69, 71
Fulham pottery, 74, 82

George IV, 68, 72
George V, 64, 70
George VI, 64
gin, 12, 14, 17
glass-bottomed mug and tankard, 30, 48
Glass Excise Act, 119, 121, 122, 126, 129
glass-making, 115
Glass Sellers' Company, 117
Gloucester Cathedral, 111
Great Eastern Steamship, 64
green men, 21

hallmarking, 35, 36, 37
Hancock, Robert, 104
Harleian Manuscript, 21
Harrison, William, 41
Haseler and Restall Ltd., 60
Henderson, David, 85
Henry VII, 42
Henry VIII, 11, 35, 40
Herold, J. G., 94, 96, 99
Hill, Graham, 70
Hogarth, 17

Holesworth, 44
hops, 11, 12
Howe, Lord Earl, 66, 72
Huguenots, 26, 27
Hurd, Jacob, 35

Imperial measure, 43, 49, 53, 54
inn, 7, 10, 21
Irish glass, 120, 126, 127, 130
iron bridge over River Wear, 62

Jacobs, J., 125
Jacobs, Lazarus, 125
Jan Steen flagon, 52, 55
Japanese influence, 95, 99, 100, 104, 114
jasper, 75, 76, 77
Jervis, Sir John (Earl St. Vincent), 66
Johnson, Dr. Samuel, 17
Julius Caesar, 9

Kakiemon, 99, 100, 104, 114
Kidder, John, 29
Kinloch, George, 62
Kunckel glass, 123

lacy pattern, 127
Lambeth, 82
Lamerie, Paul de, 31
Leeds, 69, 84
Lichfield Cathedral, 111
lids:
    domed, 27, 28, 35, 37, 50, 51
    flat, 28, 30, 37, 40, 41, 42, 50
    serrated, 40, 41, 42, 50, 51, 55
    stepped, 24, 26
lily-pad glass, 129

Lincoln Cathedral, 90
Liverpool, 103, 106, 109, 114
livery pot, 13, 31
London glass, 125
London Bridge, 64
Longfellow, 14
Longton Hall, 109, 110
Lowestoft, 103, 110, 111, 113
lustreware, 71, 72, 84, 89

Magna Carta, 10
Maiolica, 81, 84
Maling Pottery, 84
Mansell, Sir Robert, 116
Martinware, 73, 81, 86, 103
Mary, Queen, 70
May, J. and J., 62, 65, 92
Mayflower, 14, 63, 90
mead, 20, 22
measures, 44, 46, 49, 53, 54, 55
Meissen, 94, 95, 96, 99, 100, 102
Mennecy, 96, 99
merrie pin, 13, 23
Mesopotamia, 9
Milchglas (milk glass), 124, 126
miniatures, 68, 73
Minton, 109, 112
Mocha ware, 83, 84, 86
monasteries, 10, 11
Morris, William, 73, 120
mug defined, 53
mutchkin, 53

Nailsea glass, 125, 127
Napoleon, 66
Nelson, 63, 66, 67
Newcastle glass, 125, 129
New Hall, 101, 112

Noah, 9, 20

Odd Fellows and Foresters, 71
old ale standard, 43
old English wine standard, 44, 53
opaline glass, 124
opaque-white glass, 124, 125, 126

Pasteur, Louis, 16
pearlware, 85
peg tankard, 13, 23, 25, 133
peg, to take down a, 13, 23
Penn, William, 16
Perlin, Etienne, 19
pewter contents, 43, 59
pewterers, 43
Pewterers Company, 40, 44
Phillips, Captain Mark, 65, 92
pilgrims, 17, 90
Pilkington, 91
Pinxton, 109
Pliny, the elder, 9
Plymouth, 97, 100, 101, 102, 112
P.M.C. (Sheffield Ltd.), 59, 60
Poole Pottery, 91
port, 12
porter, 14, 21
Pratt, Felix, 72, 83, 88
pressed glass, 16, 21, 127, 129, 132, 133, 134
Primitive Methodist Jubilee, Chapel Tunstall, 11
pub, 7, 9, 14
pub signs, 10, 21

Queen Anne, 26, 27, 31
Queensware, 86, 90

railway subjects, 67
Ravenscroft, George, 116, 117, 118, 120
Raven's Head, 118
redware, 84, 85
repairs, silver, 36, 37
Restoration, the, 20, 25, 35
Rhineland stoneware, 23, 41, 52, 74, 79, 81
Richard II, 10
Ridgway, 110
River Severn, 112
Rockingham, 110
Rodney, Admiral, 62
Roman glass, 115
Roman pewter, 40
Rose, John, 112
Rudolph II, 122
rummers, 121

Sadler, J., 19, 61
Sadler, James and Sons, 91, 109
Savoy Glass House, 116
St. Cloud, 96, 99, 100
St. Mary's School, Birkenhead, 111
St. Paul, 20
St. Peter's Collegiate Church (Wolverhampton), 111
Sanderson, Robert, 31
Sandwich Glass Factory, 16, 127
Saxons, 7, 10, 11
Schofield, John, 29
Scottish laver, 55
Scottish capacity, 54
Sèvres, 98, 101, 102

sgraffiato, 82, 85
Shakespeare, 17, 18, 20, 70
sherry, 12, 121
slag glass, 134
slipware, 80, 82
Smith, Kirkby & Co., 44
Smith, Rev. Sydney, 10
South New Jersey glass, 128
Spode, 84, 108
sporting themes, 70, 72
Sprimont, Nicholas, 102
Stacey, 44
Standish, Miles, 14, 16
sterling silver, 35, 36
Sterne, Lawrence, 70
Stiegel, 128, 129
Stitzen, 45
stoneware, 74, 75, 76, 77, 79, 81, 82, 84, 85, 86, 87, 90
Storr, Paul, 31
Stourbridge, 125
Studio Pottery, 73, 86
Styles, Alex, 31, 33
Sunderland, 69, 129
'tanggard pots", 18, 22
tankard defined, 7, 22
tappit hens, 12, 49, 50, 53, 54, 56
tavern mugs and tankards, 43, 47, 48, 52, 54, 74, 83, 121, 131, 133
thumbpieces, 23, 28, 40, 41, 50, 51, 52, 53, 54, 55, 56, 94
thumbs up, 14
"tigerware", 33
Toby jugs, 69, 70, 71, 72, 73, 78, 79, 83, 85, 103, 134
Tom Brown's Schooldays, 20

143

tortoise shell ware, 84
touchmarks, 56, 57, 58
transfer-printing, 61, 83, 84, 108, 109
Tristram Shandy, 70
Tschirnhaus, 96
tulip shape, 48, 51
tuppenny, 14
Turner, John, 77, 80, 86, 87, 112

Union Flint Glass Works, 130
Venetian glass, 116, 119
Verzelini, Jacope, 116
Vickers, I., 44
Victoria, Queen, 66, 67, 68
Vincennes, 96, 99

Wardle and Matthews Ltd., 59
Washington, George, 16
Wedgwood, Josiah I, 61, 75, 76, 112
Wedgwood, company, 72, 75, 84, 90, 91, 114
Wellington, 63, 67, 110
Wemyss ware, 89, 91
Whieldon, 72, 82
Whitefriars, 134
William the Conqueror, 42
willow pattern, 103
wine, 10, 12, 14, 20, 22, 25
Wistar, Caspar, 128
Wolstenholme, 44
Wood, Enoch, 72
Wood, Ralph I, 71 72
Wood, Ralph II, 72
Wood, Ralph, pottery, 79, 83
Worcester, 100, 101, 103, 104, 105, 106, 107, 108, 112, 114

Worshipful Company of Goldsmiths, 13
"wriggled work", 40, 41, 42, 50, 51